THE
EXPULSION *of*
the JESUITS *from*
LATIN AMERICA

Borzoi Books ON LATIN AMERICA

General Editor
LEWIS HANKE
COLUMBIA UNIVERSITY

THE
EXPULSION *of*
the JESUITS *from*
LATIN AMERICA

❖❖❖❖❖❖❖❖❖❖

EDITED WITH AN INTRODUCTION BY

Magnus Mörner

Queens College,
The City University
of New York

New York: Alfred·A·Knopf

L. C. catalog card number: 64-23730

THIS IS A BORZOI BOOK,

PUBLISHED BY ALFRED A. KNOPF, INC.

Copyright © 1965 by Alfred A. Knopf, Inc.

FIRST EDITION

SECOND PRINTING MAY 1967

Dedicated to my friend and colleague
ROBERT N. BURR

Acknowledgments

I received the invitation to prepare this volume from Professor Lewis Hanke, who has been most helpful and encouraging during the whole arduous period of preparation. My thanks are also due to the students of his Colloquium on Latin American History at Columbia University in New York who read and criticized the manuscript in April 1964.

When preparing my previous studies on Jesuit history in Latin America I have always met with the greatest helpfulness and comprehension on the part of the Jesuit historians themselves. This time, I am very much obliged to the Rev. Father John F. Bannon, S.J., for having read and scrutinized the manuscript.

As Swedish, not English, is my mother tongue I have had to rely on translators for assistance in the preparation of the excerpts from Spanish and Portuguese texts. My thanks are due to Mrs. Denise Biblarz, Miss Belinda Brundage, Miss Eva van Ditmar, and Mrs. Ana María Moog Rodrigues.

MAGNUS MÖRNER

Contents

III   THE EXPULSION OF THE JESUITS FROM BRAZIL

IV   THE EXPULSION OF THE JESUITS FROM SPANISH AMERICA

V   THE AFTERMATH OF THE EXPULSION

THE
EXPULSION *of*
the JESUITS *from*
LATIN AMERICA

Introduction

The expulsion of the Jesuits from Portuguese America in 1759 and from Spanish America in 1767 were governmental actions that profoundly shocked colonial society. It is difficult to find any other single event of the same magnitude in the course of Latin-American history between the Conquest and the Emancipation.

Why did the expulsion of the members of one of the religious orders mean so much? The answer lies partly in undeniable facts. In the field of education the Jesuits played a dominant role. Their missions among the Indians were numerous and well organized. Thus the consequences of their expulsion were bound to be most important in both of these spheres. The expulsion of the Jesuits is not merely a question of facts, however. It is also, to an extraordinary degree, a question of myths brought into being by the extensive propaganda of both the Jesuits and their adversaries. Because of these myths, the role of some mysterious forces culminating in the act of expulsion has been greatly enhanced by both contemporary and modern writers. Consequently, the results produced by the expulsion have also been interpreted in terms of these same myths so that the whole process has been magnified, thus acquiring a superfactual dimension.

In the history of the Jesuits in Latin America and their expulsion, the facts and the myths are interlaced to a degree that makes it extremely difficult to make a clear distinction between them. Indeed, impartial historical research has as yet only begun to grapple with this important task. Moreover, sometimes the contemporary myths such as those about the hidden gold mines and the Indian puppet emperor of the Jesuit missions in Paraguay probably helped shape events.

What makes the history of the Jesuits in Latin America and their expulsion particularly complicated, finally, is the difficulty of assessing its relative importance within a European and global context. One of the main characteristics of the Jesuit Order is its centralized, international structure. Therefore everything affecting one part of the immensely farflung field of activities of the Jesuits may affect the others. For that reason, the chain of events leading to the expulsion of the Jesuits from country after country, empire after empire, ending in the suppression of the order by the Pope in 1773 is composed of the most heterogeneous elements, ranging from moral theology and political law to practices of commerce, geographically comprising events which took place in China, Martinique, and Paraguay as well as those which occurred in the royal courts of Europe. The history of the Jesuits in Latin America is only in part a Latin-American subject, and the expulsion in particular was set in motion by metropolitan agencies because of motives of their own. On the other hand, the Jesuits' Latin-American record, and the myths, undoubtedly constitute one of the most explosive elements which led to the universal reaction against the order.

In 1534 the Basque noble Ignatius of Loyola, who was both a realist and a mystic, brought together six of his fellow students from Paris in a group which was destined to become the core of the order for the purpose of undertaking a mission in the Holy Land. These plans had to be dropped, but in 1540 the founding of the Society of Jesus was confirmed by the Pope to promote both home and overseas missions. The home enterprise of the Jesuits was the starting point for their great contribution toward stopping the Protestant advance. Thus this religious activity also became a political instrument and therefore highly controversial. By means of their overseas missions, the Jesuits were to play an important political role within the European expansion in Asia, the Americas, and Africa. Sometimes they based their activity on the support of native rulers, as in Japan in the late sixteenth century and in the Mogul Empire and China in the early seventeenth century. Sometimes their missions among the natives grew so populous, wealthy, and well-organized that they became important factors in strategy and policy. This above all was the case with the famous Jesuit missions among the Guaraní Indians of the Upper River Plate region. But to some extent it was also true with regard to the rest of their missions in South America, Mexico, and the Philippines, as well as with the Canadian missions of the French Jesuits of the seventeenth century.

The explanation of the successes of the Jesuits in their mission activities and also of their commitments in political and economic affairs lies in their principles of recruitment, training, and organization. Only men of sound judgment, good character, energy, and perfect health were to be admitted to the order; if possible they were to be cultured and intelligent as well. If these conditions could be met by a candidate, an aristocratic or rich background would be an additional asset. The Jesuit Order has paid much more attention to the training of its members than any other religious order. After two years of probation, the novice takes simple monastic vows to become a member of the order. If suited for theoretical studies, he pursues such studies for about a dozen years, after which he is ordained. After a new probation period, most Jesuits become so-called *Coadjutores espirituales*. Only the real elite become the *Professi* who, strictly speaking, constitute the order. Only they take, in addition to the three solemn vows, the famous "Jesuit vow" always to be prepared for duty in the service of the Pope. There is also the most humble category of the order, the lay brothers. The Jesuits do not confine themselves to monasteries. They live and work in missions or in smaller residences, colleges, and novitiates, where they engage in teaching. All members of the order within a certain district constitute a province under a provincial. He has a number of advisers (*Consultores*) whom he must consult on all important questions and who, at the same time, watch his conduct, being able to report on him to Rome. A similar control system exists on all levels of the Jesuit hierarchy. Every third year a Provincial Congregation within each province is called to elect a representative to be sent to the General in Rome, and all these Jesuits meet in the Eternal City as a *Congregatio Procuratorum* under the chairmanship of the Father General. If the General dies or some other extraordinarily important event occurs, this body has

to decide whether a General Congregation consisting of
(among others) all the Provincials should be convened.
Only this latter assembly is able to make alterations in the
constitutions of the order. It elects the General for life
and also his *Assistentes*—his advisers with reference to districts consisting of several provinces. After 1608 there
were five such *Assistenciæ:* Italy, Germany, Spain, Portugal, and France. The authority of the General is far-
reaching. Every Jesuit, no matter to which grade he
belongs, can be dismissed by the General if found unsuita-
ble. Such ex-Jesuits have often become the most fanatical
foes of the order. The centralized character of this international organization has not remained unchallenged. In spite
of the violent opposition, mainly from nationalistic Spanish Jesuits in the late sixteenth century who wanted a de-
centralization of the executive, Father General Claudio
Aquaviva (1581-1615) was able to maintain Loyola's principles and to stabilize the whole organization.

As a *leitmotiv* in the whole structure of the order runs
the demand for strict obedience to superiors. At the same
time there functions within the order an ingenious system
of division of power and mutual control, not unlike the one
within the Communist organization. Jesuits in administrative posts are frequently changed. In 1594 the General Congregation laid down in principle that the purpose of the
order, to spread Faith, would be prejudiced and the order
itself exposed to danger if it engaged in political matters.
Very early, however, the Jesuits aimed at winning the support of powerful people for their spiritual apostolate. This
aim was certainly a natural one in the times when the principle of *Cujus regio ejus religio* was generally accepted.
The Jesuits now became the favorite confessors of princes
and nobles because of their excellent training and often aristocratic background. From this the step was not a long
one to allowing themselves to be used to perform political
services. As we shall see, this political involvement of the
Jesuits, well illustrated by the fact that the confessors of
the Bourbon kings of both France and Spain were usually
Jesuits, was to become a most important factor in bringing
about the downfall of the order.

Their vow prohibiting ownership of private property

did not prevent the Jesuits from devoting great attention to economic and financial matters. This was completely in line with their realistic approach to all problems, and because of their excellent administrative system they were more successful in this field than any other body. The starting point of their economy was the same as that of other orders: contributions from sympathizers. Like the monastic orders, they invested much of their fortune in land. But the Jesuit Order was a child of the era of commercial capitalism, and its members did not always observe the medieval prohibition against taking interest. As bankers and enterprisers they made, in fact, a pioneering contribution.[1] If some Jesuit establishment or province got into economic trouble, the centralization of the order enabled it to be aided. These economic activities, however, were likely to raise suspicions and exaggerated ideas about the wealth of the Jesuits, thus becoming an important element in the anti-Jesuit feelings which were to undermine the mighty position of the order.

To some extent the heterogeneous activities of the Jesuits all over the world *Ad Maiorem Dei Gloriam* were facilitated by a rather flexible attitude in the fields of divine worship and moral theology. As a result of their compromise with East-Indian and Chinese traditions, their missions in the Orient flourished greatly. Finally, however, the so-called Malabarese and Chinese rites were solemnly condemned by Rome, a move which brought a considerable loss of prestige for the order. The ethics presented by some Jesuit theologians also offered a curious image of compromise. According to the probabilist doctrine of the Jesuits, if one is doubtful as to the obligation of moral law in a given case, one may safely follow a "truly probable opinion"—an opinion based on a recognized theological authority, even if the contrary opinion may look even more probable. It is natural that many fellow theologians, and some Jesuits, found such a doctrine suspect and felt that it

---

[1] Cf. the discussion between H. M. Robertson (*Aspects of the Rise of Economic Individualism*, Cambridge, 1933) and the Jesuit J. Brodrick (*The Economic Morals of the Jesuits*, London, 1934).

lent itself to abuse. Another controversial theological field was the relation between human free will and divine grace. While the French Jansenists of the seventeenth century interpreted the teachings of Saint Augustine as a doctrine of predestination, which caused them to be condemned by the Pope, the Jesuits were inclined to stress the importance of free will. Father Luis Molina tried to reconcile the two contrary concepts, which brought upon him and the order the implacable hatred of other theologians, particularly members of the Augustinian and, to a degree, the Dominican Orders. The Jesuits branded all their opponents "Jansenists." As a result of their influence the works of the great Augustinian theologian Cardinal Enrico Noris were prohibited by the Inquisition in Spain in 1747 in spite of protests by the Vatican. The tension between the Jesuits and the other orders became public. As Jesuits by their own rules were not allowed to accept bishoprics and similar posts, unless by way of exception, they lacked an episcopal support they would otherwise have possessed. In Spain the hard feelings of the orders against the Jesuits increased when a Jesuit author, Father José Francisco de Isla, was unwise enough to publish a satirical novel (in 1758) about Fray Gerundio, the prototype of the Castilian monk.

The Jesuits, although not always correctly, were generally considered to be ultramontane, i.e., supporters of the authority of the Pope as opposed to the nationalistic tendencies within the Church. In France the Gallicanists therefore joined the Jansenists in the struggle against the hated followers of Loyola. This violent anti-Jesuit campaign was to be carried to a successful end a hundred years later by the partisans of the Enlightenment. In Spain such sixteenth-century Jesuits as Francisco Suárez and Juan de Mariana in their works on political philosophy defended the rights of the people in relation to the monarch, a conception based on scholastic ideas sometimes called the Populist doctrine. Long before Rousseau, Suárez formulated the contract theory of the origin of society. Father Mariana, for his part, even defended the right of the people to murder a tyrant. It is not surprising that enlightened eighteenth-century despotism should find such thinking extremely dangerous.

The expansion of the order was rapid. When Loyola died in 1556 there were already 1,000 Jesuits divided into 12 provinces. When Aquaviva died in 1615 there were 13,112 members of the order and no less than 32 European and overseas provinces. By the middle of the eighteenth century the number of Jesuits had almost doubled.

Parallel with the expansion in quantitative terms, a qualitative decline set in after the death of Father Aquaviva. The dedication gradually slackened, the authority of the General diminished, the national rivalries within the framework of the order grew, and the cases of violation of the vows became more frequent. For some Jesuits the economic and political commitments became ends instead of means. Such conditions, even if only partially visible from outside, were apt to provide the foes of the order with fuel. The commercial manipulations of Father Antoine Lavalette in the French West Indies were the immediate cause of the downfall of the order in France in 1764. The moral decline of the Jesuits should not be overrated, however. In the context of the eighteenth-century Church, itself infected with the worldliness and doubts characteristic of what we call the enlightened era, the Jesuit Order remained a body of higher quality both on a personal and an organizational level than other ecclesiastical bodies. Indeed, what concentrated the attacks upon the Jesuit Order was its remaining strength rather than its growing weaknesses.

What brought the Jesuit Order to the fore of public attention was not only the heterogeneous activities of the Jesuits as such. To a great extent it was the publicity Jesuits themselves spread about their order. Perhaps no other religious body has been capable of such systematic information activity as the Jesuits, while at the same time their secretiveness on certain points left the field open to wild speculation. The Jesuit propaganda created widespread admiration, but it also gave rise to exaggerated ideas about the power and achievements of the order, which in turn caused hostility in various quarters. The frequent and systematic correspondence and report-writing within the order was a natural consequence of the centralization of the organization. The annual reports that each Jesuit establishment and province was supposed to prepare, after having been "cleaned" of their secret parts, were often published or copied to stimulate the recruitment of new Jesuits and to promote "public relations" in general. The Jesuit reports from exotic mission fields published in French as *Lettres édifiantes et curieuses* and in German as *Der neue Weltbott* were among the best sellers of the eighteenth century.

Besides the publication of the reports there were also a great number of Jesuits engaged in historical writing on the different provinces of the order, sometimes directly appointed for the task by their superiors. The superior intellectual quality of the Jesuits guaranteed the comparatively high level of all this writing. It was the informative Jesuit literature that first provided Europe with the detailed knowledge of the Far East that helped to create exoticism, an important element within the Enlightenment. The Jesuit reports from Brazil and Canada were, however unintentionally, to constitute some of the main ingredients for the conception of the Noble Savage, best known to us in Rousseau's version.

Headed by Manoel de Nóbrega, the Jesuits began their mission in Brazil in 1549, a few years after Francisco Xavier had started the Jesuit overseas missions in India. Their activities as missionaries, teachers, and political advisers in the rudimentary Brazilian society are difficult to exaggerate. The history of the Jesuits in Brazil is highly dramatic, with the seventeenth-century missionary, preacher, and politician Father António Vieira as its principal actor. The conflict between the efforts of the Jesuits to keep the Indians protected and isolated from the rest of the community in their mission villages (*aldeias*) and the colonists' demand for Indian labor to be used without restrictions constitute the main theme. When the Jesuits made public a papal bull condemning Indian slavery they were expelled from São Paulo in 1640. After that Maranhão and Pará in northeastern Brazil became the center of the conflict. During the late 1650's the Jesuit rule in this region was virtually complete, but in 1661 the missionaries were expelled by the embittered colonists. They were soon able to return and their pro-Indian policy once again won the approval of the King.

In 1684 they were again turned out by their foes, only to return again. Even if from then on they had to share the expanse of Amazonas with other orders, the Jesuit mission remained the principal one. In the eighteenth century they exercised both religious and temporal administration in twenty-eight wealthy and well-kept missions situated along the Madeira River. In the wake of the Treaty of 1750 these missions, as well as those of the Spanish Jesuits on the River Uruguay, attracted the attention of the new *de facto* ruler of Portugal, Sebastião José de Carvalho, later Count of Oeiras and Marquis of Pombal. While the Spanish Jesuits' opposition to the treaty provoked Pombal's anger, a brother of his who had been entrusted with the boundary adjustment in Amazonas clashed with the Jesuit missionaries there. In 1755 the Jesuits were deprived of their temporal authority over the Indians, whose complete liberty was decreed at the same time. A couple of years later the first group of missionaries was deported from Amazonas. By 1759 all Jesuits had been expelled from Portuguese dominions. Only a few badly treated Jesuits remained imprisoned in Lisbon. With the expulsion of about 500 Jesuits, the Brazilian community lost most of its teachers and missionaries. But the expulsion was also a consequence of events which occurred on European soil. The final decree of expulsion was, in fact, based mainly on alleged Jesuit participation in an aristocratic conspiracy against the Portuguese king.

So far as Spanish America is concerned, the Jesuits were much slower in arriving there than in Portuguese America; nor were they to play so dominant a role. The "spiritual conquest" of the central parts of New Spain and Peru was largely the work of Franciscans, Dominicans, Augustinians, and Mercedarians. The first Jesuit missions in Spanish America, in Florida and on the Atlantic coast farther north in the late 1560's, were failures. When the Jesuits made their appearance in the different territories of Spanish America they were, for a long time, mostly active as teachers, and their colleges attracted an elite of Spanish-American youth. "Specialists in education with an unprecedented reputation abroad, the followers of Ignatius Loyola dominated the sphere of higher education in all but the royal and pontifical universities." [2] They also systematically prepared themselves for missionary undertakings, adopting the method already recommended by colonial legislation of gathering the Indians in permanent mission villages called *reducciones*, the counterparts of the *aldeias* of Brazil. The economy of a *reducción* according to the laws was based on a kind of collective organization with roots in the past of the Andean Indians. The obligations of the Indians and the other aspects of community life were also outlined in detail in the legislation. Thus the Jesuit missions were not as unique as they are often represented. What was extraordinary was the degree to which they were able to apply the principles which had already been laid down for the Indian policy of both Church and Crown.

While the village of Juli in Alto Perú (Bolivia), put in charge of the Jesuits in 1576, as well as, possibly, the *aldeias* of Brazil, served as a model for later undertakings, no Jesuit missions were to be so famous as those among the Guaraní Indians of "Paraguay." [3] In the eighteenth century there were thirty of them, situated along and between the rivers of Upper Paraná and Uruguay with a total of 100,-000 people, and they were better organized than any others. But, in spite of all the innumerable works and polemics that have been devoted to their "theocratical communism," "Utopian socialism," and so on, their internal organization was not unique. Both other Jesuit missions and those of other orders in Spanish America offer a similar picture. What gave the Jesuit missions, and particularly those among the Guaraní, their dramatic character was the result of two circumstances: the conflict between the Jesuit demand to manage their missions without interference from outside and the colonist demand for Indian labor, and the connection between the peripherical missions and the border question.[4] The Indians' obligation to perform work for their

---

[2] John Tate Lanning, *Academic Culture in the Spanish Colonies* (London, 1940), p. 21.

[3] The Jesuit province of Paraguay ("*Paracuaria*") comprised the whole region of the River Plate. Only some of the Guaraní missions lay within the borders of the present republic of Paraguay.

[4] Magnus Mörner, *The Political and Economic Activities of*

encomenderos—colonists privileged to collect tribute the Indians would otherwise pay to the Crown—was systematically opposed by the Jesuits. This attitude in a delicate matter caused them to be the subject of much hatred, especially as their opposition to the colonists in this question was often accompanied by trade competition. In Paraguay the conflict—at times an armed conflict—between the Jesuit missions and Paraguayan colonists was largely a question of competition in the export of Paraguayan tea, the region's only important product. It was the Paraguayan rivals who put into circulation the unfounded rumors about hidden gold mines in the Jesuit missions.

Herbert Bolton has stressed the border function of the missions and the role played by the missionaries as Indian "agents" of the Crown.[5] His observations were based on the mission activities of the order on the west coast of New Spain and in Lower California where Fathers Eusebio Kino and Juan María de Salvatierra led the "spiritual conquest" during the end of the seventeenth and the first years of the eighteenth century, as well as on the later Franciscan mission in California. But the Jesuits until 1767 were also active in several mission districts on the Portuguese border in South America. Jesuit missions represented Spain on the shores of Orinoco, in the southern plains of modern Colombia, in the jungles of Amazonas (where they finally succumbed to Portuguese advances), and among the Chiquito Indians in the eastern lowlands of present-day Bolivia. A close relation between mission and border can be discerned in Chile, too, where the Jesuit Luis de Valdivia for some time in the beginning of the seventeenth century was able to substitute the eternal warfare against the Araucanians with the peaceful mission approach. At about the same time, the Indians of the Jesuit missions in Upper River Plate became victims of slave hunts organized by the Brazilian half-breeds of São Paulo. In the absence of assistance from local

the Jesuits in the La Plata Region. The Hapsburg Era (Stockholm, 1953), pp. 199-201.

[5] H. E. Bolton, "The Mission as a Frontier Institution in the Spanish American Colonies," *American Historical Review*, XXIII (1917), reproduced in his *Wider Horizons of American History* (New York, London, 1939).

authorities the Jesuits finally put up an effective defense by using firearms. The slave hunters from Brazil were beaten in the Battle of Mbororé in 1641 at the very moment when Portugal broke away from its union with Spain.

This background explains how the Guaraní of the Jesuit missions from 1649 onward became a kind of privileged frontier garrison at the disposal of the Spanish authorities of Buenos Aires, a position not enjoyed by any other missions, since the other border missions were usually assisted by detachments of Spanish soldiers. The Guaraní were used not only in the frontier wars against Portugal but also against hostile Indians and against the colonists of Paraguay when the latter rose in rebellion under Antequera in the 1720's. The role of the Jesuit missionaries in these non-ecclesiastical activities was a somewhat dubious one. Officially they acted only as chaplains, but in reality their authority over the Indians was unlimited in war and peace alike.

Although the powerful position of the Jesuits and their Guaraní missions continuously increased the number of opponents and foes, it remained about the same until the middle of the eighteenth century. In 1743 they even obtained a royal confirmation of the privileged status of the missions, plus a refutation of current rumors. But eighteenth-century politics were unpredictable and the Spanish-Portuguese Treaty of 1750 arbitrarily exchanged the Spanish territory to the south of the Uruguay River with seven Jesuit missions for the Portuguese bulwark Colonia do Sacramento on the River Plate. The Jesuit protests were in vain and finally the Indians of the seven missions rose in rebellion against the orders to evacuate their homeland. But now the military potential of the Indians had been reduced, relatively speaking, and it was rather easy for the combined Spanish-Portuguese troops to inflict upon them a crushing defeat. Were the Jesuits the real culprits behind the mutiny of the former garrison? Was there an actual Jesuit State hidden in the wilds of "Paraguay"? Was this "state" a part of a universal conspiracy of the Jesuits to take control of the world? Although the responsibility of individual missionaries remains uncertain, the rest of the questions can easily be denied today on the basis of historical documentation. But it was more difficult for their contemporaries to ascertain the truth, and the rumors emanating from Paraguay undoubtedly played an important part in creating universal suspicion of the order.

The Jesuit missions of "Paraguay" and the Guaraní War no doubt provided the foes of the order in Spanish America most of their ammunition. But there were also other motives for the anti-Jesuit rumors and complaints there. Thanks to the influence they sometimes enjoyed in Madrid, the Jesuits obtained permission to send certain numbers of non-Spaniards as missionaries to America, which was otherwise strictly closed to foreigners.[6] Though these German, French, and Italian Jesuits were often very distinguished and always loyal to the Crown, their presence easily provoked nationalistic suspicions and hostility and therefore they often figured in rumors. What also caused bad blood was the opulence of the Jesuit missions and colleges in general. Envy made the conflicts with the other orders or the episcopate particularly bitter. Conflicts arising over ecclesiastical jurisdiction and the tenure of benefices were frequent in colonial Spanish America, and bishops, secular and regular clergy were often at loggerheads. But the conflict between the Jesuits of Mexico and Bishop Juan de Palafox of Puebla in the middle of the seventeenth century succeeded in seriously shaking the position of the order both in Rome and Madrid. When the proposal of Palafox's canonization was opposed by the Jesuits a hundred years later, the issue was revived, adding more fuel to the fire which was to destroy the order.

The activities of the Jesuits in Spanish America were only in part responsible for the catastrophe. The Guaraní War probably had more influence on Pombal's behavior than on that of Charles III. Circumstances and events at close range were much more important in provoking the decree of expulsion in the following year than grievances of American origin. Especially there were the so-called "Hat and Cloak riots" in March and April 1766, caused both by excessive food prices and by the unpopularity of

---

[6] See Lázaro de Aspurz, *La aportación extranjera a las misiones españolas del Patronato Regio* (Madrid, 1946).

the Italian ministers of Charles III. A prohibition for the
Madrileños to wear their common broad-brimmed hats
and long capes gave the signal for rioting. The order's foes
afterwards claimed, however, that the Jesuits had incited
the masses. The effect of the expulsion of more than 2,200
Jesuits no doubt was profound in Spanish America, both in
the missionary and teaching fields, although there were
many more friars and priests to take over their tasks than
had been the case in Brazil. The extensive material holdings
of the order were confiscated by the state.

After their expulsion most Jesuits from Spanish and
Portuguese America passed their remaining days in Italy,
often devoting their time to scholarly work and writing.
Since the suppression of the order in 1773 by the Pope, who
had been forced to this drastic measure by France, Portugal,
and Spain, they also kept together. Homesick American-
born Jesuit writers were among the first representatives of
literary nationalism in Latin America. Discussing the exiled
Jesuits of New Spain, Mariano Picón Salas states that these
"writers felt themselves Mexicans far more than citizens of
the Spanish empire that had punished and outraged them,
and in a foreign sanctuary whose inhabitants knew so little
about America, they endeavored to assert their nascent national pride and reveal to the educated world the wealth
and the interest or fascination of their land of birth." There
exists a strong temptation to connect this "Jesuitic humanism" (to borrow a term from Picón-Salas) with the rise
of nationalism as expressed by the movement for independence. Speaking about the last generation of Jesuits in New
Spain with such men as Francisco Javier Clavijero, Francisco Javier Alegre, and Andrés Cavo as its intellectual
leaders, a Mexican student of intellectual history, Bernabé
Navarro Barajas, asserts that, among the colonial writers
and philosophers, the Jesuits were "certainly those who
contributed most in establishing the ideological bases for
our emancipation." [7] But did the Jesuits also maintain rela-

---

[7] M. Picón Salas, *A Cultural History of Spanish America.
From Conquest to Independence*, trans. I. A. Leonard (Berkeley,
Los Angeles, 1963), p. 137; B. Navarro, "Los jesuítas y la Inde-

tions with the foes of Spain in the hope of provoking the emancipation of Spanish America as a kind of vengeance? Many rumors to this effect circulated at the time between the expulsion and the emancipation, and they have often appeared in historical writing. As one Jesuit scholar observes, however, it is easy to trace the origin of the rumors:

> There were two motives for attributing separatist schemes to the ex-Jesuits. The first was the abnormal fear of the Spanish government through whose emotional skies there seemed to whirl as many Jesuits as we have flying saucers; the second, the advantage accruing to the patriots by associating the names of these exiles with their independence movement.[8]

In two individual cases, however, ex-Jesuits undoubtedly belonged to the active plotters against the Spanish government in the Indies: in the case of the Peruvian Pablo Viscardo and the Chilean Juan José Godoy. That they were isolated cases has convincingly been shown by the Jesuit historian Miguel Batllori.[9] After the order had been restored by the Pope in 1814, the Jesuits soon returned to Latin America to take up their work again, although in somewhat different ways.

The historical discussion about the Jesuits in general has tended to be heated and polemical. Black and white arguments have been the rule. This has also been true about the discussion of the events leading up to the fall of the order in Portugal and Spain and the effect of this upon the society of the New World. The religious and political backgrounds of the various authors often dictated their views, at least until very recent times.

Certain aspects of the activities of the order, such as the so-called "Jesuit State of Paraguay," were sometimes judged

---

pendencia," *Abside: Revista de Cultura Mexicana*, XV (México, 1952), p. 43.

[8] Ernest J. Burrus, "Jesuit Exiles, Precursors of Mexican Independence?," *Mid-America*, XXXVI (1954), 163.

[9] *El abate Viscardo: historia y mito de la intervención de los jesuítas en la independencia de Hispanoamérica* (Caracas, 1953).

on the basis of more independent criteria, however.[1] The Guaraní community of the Jesuits was reluctantly commended in part even by such fiery opponents of the order as Voltaire, D'Alembert, and Montesquieu. In spite of the fact that they considered the Jesuits the principal representatives of hypocrisy and superstition, the "Jesuit State" appeared to the leaders of the Age of Enlightenment an admirable experiment by which European intellect proved its ability to create a society according to given plans. Favorable, almost without reservation, was the judgment on the missions of another rationalist author, the ex-Jesuit Raynal, who underlined the contrast with Spanish colonization, described in accordance with the Black Legend. Raynal's contemporary, the sober Scottish historian and churchman William Robertson, also saw something of an ideal community in the "Jesuit State"; but as his view on the Spanish Empire was surprisingly positive, the contrast offered by the "Jesuit State" was less striking. Romanticism's view of the "Jesuit State," well represented by Chateaubriand, naturally attached great importance to the religious and esthetic aspects, idealizing the subject at the cost of historical truth. The British writer Robert Southey, of the same generation, on the other hand, gave a knowledgeable account—vacillating, however, in his final judgment. From a purely liberal point of view, the "Jesuit State," as a rule conceived as a rationalistic experiment, seemed a rather dubious phenomenon. Thus the opinion expressed by Liberal writers, particularly by Latin Americans, was generally negative, underlining the lack of freedom of the Indians. On the other hand, Socialist-influenced writers have often taken a positive view of the Jesuit "experiment." The Scotsman Cunninghame Graham is one of the representatives of this trend. Characteristic of most of the writing on the "Jesuit State" until recent times has been the tendency to isolate the topic from its Spanish-American context and even from its relation with the history of the order as a whole. On such a basis it is possible

---

[1] Historiographical survey, Mörner, *The Political and Economic Activities* . . . , pp. 194-198.

to construct attractive theories or literary masterpieces but not history.

Thus the story of the expulsion of the Jesuits from the realm of Charles III has to be approached on a very broad basis and that has seldom been tried. The Spanish historians of the late nineteenth and early twentieth centuries who have dealt with the topic, Antonio Ferrer del Río, and Manuel Dánvila y Collado as well as the Frenchman François Rousseau, have chiefly dwelt on the question of Jesuit implication in the Hat and Cloak Riots against the hated Marquis of Squillace, Italian-born Secretary of State for Finances and War in the spring of 1766. That the Jesuits did not organize the riots seems to have been definitely made clear by a modern Jesuit scholar.[2]

To explain the king's anger at the Jesuits a simplistic theory has been advanced to the effect that they started rumors about the illegitimacy of his birth. Although the great historian of the papacy, Ludwig von Pastor, long ago dismissed this theory as baseless, it still manages to survive.[3] The secretive wording of the royal decree expelling the Jesuits also still puzzles many students of the topic, although explanatory documentation is not at all lacking. In the shadow of this official secretiveness "conspiracy theories" have gained strength. States Vicente de la Fuente, the author of a history of Spanish Masonry, published in 1870:

> It is without doubt today that [the Foreign Minister] Wall and the Duke of Alba led all the infamous and concealed plots which aimed at preparing the expulsion of the Jesuits in accordance with [the wishes of] English Protestantism and European freemasonry.[4]

For obvious reasons this "conspiracy theory" has been popular with many Jesuit and conservative Catholic writers; for example Vicente Sierra, in his recent *Historia de la*

---

[2] C. Eguía Ruiz, *Los jesuítas y el motín de Esquilache* (Madrid, 1947).

[3] *The History of the Popes from the Close of the Middle Ages,* trans. E. F. Peeler, XXXVII (St. Louis, Mo.), 143-150.

[4] *Historia de las sociedades secretas antiguas y modernas en España y especialmente de la francmasonería,* I (Lugo, 1870), 103.

Argentina, emphasizes that Great Britain's principal aim during the eighteenth century was to weaken Spain, and at the same time was the center of international Masonry. Therefore the anti-Jesuit conspiracies of Spanish politicians such as Ricardo Wall, Count of Aranda, Manuel de Roda, and Pedro Rodríguez de Campomanes—all of them Masons, according to Sierra—in reality served the British interests against Spain.[5] Even Salvador de Madariaga, although politically removed from Sierra's extreme rightist position, expresses somewhat similar opinions. He also maintains that it is

> . . . a curious coincidence of History that, as a result of the well-meant but mistaken endeavors of a group of Spanish enlightened despots [!], the Jesuits were driven to cooperate with the other two international brotherhoods, the Freemasons and the Jews, in the destruction of the Spanish Empire.[6]

As can be seen, Madariaga also thinks that the political activities of the exiled Jesuits against Spain were of great importance. With regard to the relation of the Jesuits with the Freemasons, either as deadly foes or, later on, as allies, it should be noticed that a modern specialist on eighteenth-century Spain calls the frequent talk about Masonry in Spain during this period "a fable . . . for which there is no contemporary evidence." [7]

Another "conspiracy theory" has also been advanced. The Spanish historian Vicente Rodríguez Casado, a Catholic writer of the Opus Dei persuasion, seeks the explanation of the expulsion in the intrigues of the former *Manteístas,* students of less means who had never been able to study at the Jesuit colleges, whose students were regularly recruited from among the rich and privileged youth. According to

---

5 *Historia de la Argentina. Fin del régimen de gobernadores y creación del Virreinato del Río de la Plata (1700-1800),* (Buenos Aires, 1959), pp. 326-335.

6 *The Fall of the Spanish American Empire* (New York, 1948), p. 283.

7 Richard Herr, *The Eighteenth-Century Revolution in Spain* (Princeton, N.J., 1958), p. 326.

this author, the majority of the men who surrounded Charles III possessed a *Manteísta* background.[8]

Other historians see the principal cause of the expulsion in the conflict between Spanish "regalism" or a nationalistic ecclesiastical policy and the "ultramontanism" of the Vatican, with which the Jesuits became identified. Ricardo Krebs Wilckens asserts that instead of being the victims of obscure intrigues the Jesuit Order succumbed in the struggle between the modern state demanding complete sovereignty and the medieval and counterreform aspirations of "ultramontanism" of subordinating the worldly interests to those of the Church.[9] Even if such a generalization might be justified, it should be kept in mind, however, that many influential Jesuits such as some of the confessors of the Spanish kings belonged to the regalist faction. One of these Jesuits was considered in the Vatican to be perhaps the main obstacle for reaching an understanding with Spain such as the one finally arrived at by the Concordat of 1753.[1]

While the Jesuit attitude on the issue of regalism and ultramontanism was thus somewhat divided, Jesuit support of the theory of the popular origin of political power was probably wholehearted enough to allow it to be entitled a "Jesuit doctrine." On this basis several recent Catholic and Jesuit authors such as Father Guillermo Furlong of Argentina have sought the cause of the fall of the Jesuits in the opposition of enlightened despotism to this doctrine. But they have also tried to prove even more. According to them, the political thinking of Suárez instead of the influence of French enlightenment was the main intellectual ferment behind the Spanish-American revolutions. This last hypothesis has been criticized, since Spanish-American universities were "cleaned" by the authorities from all teaching of the Suárez doctrine shortly after the expulsion of the Jesuits, more than forty years before emancipation.

---

[8] "Iglesia y estado en el reinado de Carlos III," *Estudios Americanos*, I (1948), 45.

[9] *El pensamiento histórico, político y económico del Conde de Campomanes* (Santiago de Chile, 1960), p. 155.

[1] Pastor, *History of the Popes*, XXXV, 63-66.

Could its vital power really have survived this staggering blow to influence the young generation of the revolution? On the other hand, the very reaction of the state against the teaching of the "Populist" Jesuit doctrine in the university seems to provide additional evidence for its importance as a motive for the expulsion in 1767. Its relative significance still remains to be assessed, however.[2]

It can hardly be expected that the different interpretations which seek to explain the causes of the expulsion on lofty intellectual and theoretical levels would provide the whole answer. This event, with its important political repercussions, must also be placed in a context of practical politics. It was the Treaty of 1750 between Spain and Portugal with its antecedents of political vision as well as of petty intrigues that placed the Jesuit missions in South America in the focus of international attention. It was also this border treaty which caused the downfall of the pro-French Spanish statesman Ensenada in 1754, soon followed by the removal of his Jesuit friend Father Rávago from the post of confessor to the king. The Treaty has often been attributed to English influence, but this is denied by a Luso-Brazilian specialist, Professor Jaime Cortesão.[3] However, the international implications of what happened in South America should not be underrated, and it is probably wise to keep the changing combinations of European power policy well in mind when analyzing the causes of the fall of the Jesuits in both Portugal and Spain.

For the rest, the historical discussion of the causes of the expulsion of the Jesuits from the Portuguese realm seems to offer somewhat less general interest than is the case with

---

[2] See, e.g., Manuel Giménez Fernández, *Las doctrinas populistas en la independencia de Hispano-América* (Sevilla, 1947), p. 575; Guillermo Furlong, *Los jesuítas y la escisión del Reino de Indias* (Buenos Aires, 1960), and other works of the same author; theory criticized by Charles C. Griffin in Arthur P. Whitaker (ed.), *Latin America and the Enlightenment*, 2nd ed. (Ithaca, N.Y., 1961), pp. 124-125. See also the discussion between C. W. Arnade and B. W. Diffie in "Causes of Spanish-American Wars of Independence," *Journal of Inter-American Studies*, II (1960), 130-131, 141-144.

[3] His introduction to *Alexandre de Gusmão e o tratado de Madri*, Vol. 1 (Rio de Janeiro, 1950), pp. 7-9.

regard to Spain. To a great extent and with considerable justification, the discussion is likely to concentrate upon the despotic personality of the Marquis of Pombal and the motivations of his hatred for the Society of Jesus. While Pombal's desire to eliminate the political influence of the Jesuits in order to strengthen his own regime is usually emphasized, a Portuguese historian, the Viscount of Carnaxide instead points out important financial and economic aspects of his action. While an economic decline began in Brazil about 1760, the financial difficulties of the government increased even earlier as a result of the Lisbon earthquake and the Guaraní War. What Pombal aimed at by his action was to obtain the Jesuit properties which he certainly overrated, the Portuguese author observes.[4]

While Pombal painted life in the Jesuit missions in very somber colors in his famous pamphlet "Relação Abbreviada," later descriptions of the *aldeias* have usually been favorable to the fathers and their civilizing mission, abruptly ended by the expulsion. In the light of modern anthropological and sociological research, however, the tremendous cultural change forced upon the natives by the Jesuit missionaries might be considered a controversial solution. For that reason, Gilberto Freyre, the famous Brazilian sociologist, concludes that the influence of the Jesuit missions on the natives—in spite of all their good intentions—

> . . . was a harmful one. Quite as harmful as that of the colonists, their antagonists, who, animated by economic interest or pure sensuality, saw in the Indian only a voluptuous female to be taken or a rebellious slave to be subjugated and exploited. . . .[5]

If a modern sociologist may be disposed to consider the benevolent "segregation system" of the missions an obstacle to social integration, the fear of eighteenth-century authorities that the missions constituted a state within the State will perhaps seem more understandable.

---

[4] Visconde de Carnaxide, *Brasil na administração pombalina. Economia e política externa* (São Paulo . . . , 1940), p. 161.

[5] *The Masters and the Slaves (Casa Grande & Senzala)*, trans. S. Putnam (New York, 1956), p. 109.

While the South American background thus lends itself to somewhat differing interpretations, Pombal's efforts of using the alleged conspiracy of the Tavora family against the king as a pretext for his action against the order can hardly be taken seriously by modern historians. The horrifying brutality of Pombal's action also works in favor of the victims. The burning at the stake of the old Jesuit missionary Gabriel Malagrida by the Inquisition, at the orders of Pombal, even produced mixed feelings in that archenemy of the order, Voltaire.[6]

The discussion of the motives of the expulsion in both Portugal and Spain has its natural counterpart in a discussion of its consequences. And in this case, by way of distinction from the complicated web of causes, it might be possible to distinguish Spanish and Portuguese America from the mother countries. In spite of the persisting contrasts between Liberal and Catholic interpretations, the general impression of most works dealing with the effects of the acts of expulsion of 1759 and 1767 is that of immediate catastrophe, both in the missionary and education fields. As a representative of this traditional view we may well choose Salvador de Madariaga, who states that

> The expulsion of the Jesuits was unfortunate for Spain. True the order had, and has, the usual share of human defects; but, as in the case of the Jews and of the Moriscos, these defects were more than compensated for by qualities of hard work, efficiency, and culture which a country more wisely governed would not have thrown away. . . . The loss was even greater in the Indies. Irreparable damage was caused to the Missions of Paraguay, which were all but sacked and destroyed by the get-rich-quick, unscrupulous officials, with much hardship to the Indians. The loss in educational institutions was even greater than in the case of Spain.[7]

As far as the missions are concerned, this somber conclusion may grow out of admiration for the work of the Jesuit fathers. On the contrary, it may also serve for judg-

---

[6] Madariaga, *Fall*, p. 272.

[7] Madariaga, *Fall*, pp. 281-282.

ing the missionary work as entirely superficial. It would be easy to exemplify both trends. Recent research, however, tends to favor a more moderate interpretation. It is an easily proved fact that the famous missions of "Paraguay" suffered only a gradual decline after the Jesuits had left in 1768. And not all Guaraní Indians forgot the abilities they had acquired from their Jesuit masters but, thanks to these same qualities, were easily absorbed into colonial society. A student of this phenomenon affirms that the documentation he has gathered on the Guaraní of the former Jesuit missions "is sufficient to end the widespread fable of the missionary Indians returning to the forest." At the same time the thirty missions declined on account of the desertions, the same circumstance "indirectly promoted the progress of other parts of the Viceroyalty [of Río de la Plata] which absorbed the natives civilized by the religious." [8]

The effect of the Jesuit expulsion upon colonial education has also proved to be a more controversial matter than it used to appear in the light of modern research on the role of the Enlightenment in Latin-American intellectual and university life. On one hand, it is true that many learned Jesuits of the eighteenth century were themselves bearers of the new thoughts, i.e., of what is sometimes called the Catholic Enlightenment.[9] The thinking of Descartes and Leibnitz was taught by Jesuit professors in Quito and Buenos Aires, and other Jesuits in Mexico, for instance Francisco Xavier Clavijero, were even more advanced. On the other hand, the reforms which really opened the gates of the Spanish-American universities for new currents of thought did not take place until after 1767. It was then that chairs of ecclesiastical history, of patristic literature, and of other "modern" disciplines were introduced in colonial universities, thus inflicting a defeat on the upholders of scholasticism and Aristotelianism. It would be difficult to deny that there was some correlation be-

---

[8] José M. Mariluz Urquijo, "Los guaraníes después de la expulsión de los jesuítas," *Estudios Americanos*, VI (1953), 328.

[9] See, e.g., Mario Góngora, "Estudios sobre el Galicanismo y la Ilustración católica en América Española," *Revista Chilena de Historia y Geografía*, No. 125 (1957), pp. 133-134.

tween the Jesuit expulsion and the university reform in Spanish America. That the Jesuits had been trying to monopolize higher education in a rather ruthless way is stressed by John Tate Lanning in his learned account of the University of San Carlos in Guatemala, but he also observes:

> There was so much scrambling for the wealth left behind [by the expelled Jesuits] that the historian, rather than the creole of 1767, has been the man to appreciate fully the fantastic gap the expulsion created in the Indies. The many Jesuit schools, colleges, and minor universities—eight of these—were never effectively replaced under the empire.[1]

In the case of the Portuguese empire the effects of the expulsion on the educational system seems to have been very different in the metropolis and in Brazil. While education in Portugal was reformed according to the new currents of thought from 1759 onward, in Brazil, which did not possess any university of its own, according to Pedro Calmon,

> The Enlightenment . . . disorganized the existing education, without improving it [or] without even substituting it for another superior system. The Jesuit schools being closed, numerous classes of grammar and philosophy soon disintegrated and were completely discontinued around 1760. . . . Jesuit pedagogy was silenced and its absence continued to be observed and lamented; whereas in Portugal, much was expected of the profound university reform. It did not benefit Brazil![2]

And what was the reaction of the colonial community when suddenly confronted with the condemnation of its favorite teachers and confessors? Although the external reactions throughout Latin America are rather easy to trace, current generalizations differ from "indifference" to "mixed feelings" or "profound shock." For the Spanish

---

[1] *The University in the Kingdom of Guatemala* (Ithaca, N.Y., 1955), p. 97.
[2] *História do Brasil*, Vol. 3 (São Paulo, 1941), pp. 241-243.

conservative thinker Ramiro de Maeztu, "the fact is that
the expulsion of Jesuits caused such a horror for Spain
among many Criollo families that even after six generations it is still noticeable." [3] From such extreme statements the step is a short one to list the memories of the
expulsion as one of the main factors of the downfall of the
Spanish empire. With his usual literary talent Madariaga expresses this view of the importance of the shock:

> Suddenly, from this Spain of the sceptre and the Cross,
> from the very King of Spain heir to Ferdinand and
> Isabel came that most tangible proof of Voltaire's
> philosophy: "Out with the Jesuits." On that day, the
> King of Spain with his own hands cut the most solid
> link between his Crown and his subjects overseas. [4]

To this psychological effect, as previously stated, Madariaga and other authors add the importance of the political
activities of the ex-Jesuit Viscardo and other "Patriots"
among the exiled. Charles Griffin summarizes the present state of research, however, when he says that

> Without meaning to do so, it is possible that the politi-
> cal principles of the Bourbon monarchs of Spain may
> have helped promote revolution in America. The ex-
> pulsion of the Jesuits has been held by some to have
> alienated many subjects of the crown, though the po-
> litical activities in this field of the exiled Jesuits them-
> selves seem to have been very minor. [5]

Viscardo maintained in his famous *Lettre aux Espag-
nols-Américains* that the "expulsion and ruin of the Jesuits
had to all appearances no other cause than the fame of
their riches. . . ." [6] If this was so, the confiscation of the
properties of the order in both Spanish America and Brazil
soon revealed the true extent of the Jesuit holdings, which
was not really sensational if judged against the background

---

[3] *Defensa de la Hispanidad*, 5th ed. (Madrid, 1946), pp. 39-40.
[4] Madariaga, *Fall*, p. 282.
[5] In Whitaker, *Latin America and the Enlightenment* . . . , p.
136.
[6] *Lettre* . . . (Philadelphia, 1799), p. 28 (reproduced by Batllori, *op. cit.*).

of current myths. Therefore, the discussion of this aspect of the history of the expulsion has generally favored a pro-Jesuit interpretation. However, the detailed inventories of the colleges and missions at the moment of the expulsion provide the starting point for the study of a redistribution of property that probably had far-reaching consequences. To which categories did the purchasers of Jesuit properties from the *Juntas de Temporalidades* belong? Which were the economic, social, and perhaps political consequences of the redistribution? This research has hardly been initiated, a study of this aspect of Jesuit history in Mendoza in present Argentina being one of the few exceptions.[7]

Almost all the writers who, from one viewpoint or another, have dealt with the expulsion of the Jesuits from Spanish and Portuguese America have done so without seriously considering more than one of the two regions. Nevertheless, a comparison might be most useful and—indeed—necessary to obtain a true perspective. Robert Ricard advances some very interesting points of view:

> While we see in the Spanish empire a strong predominance of the Mendicant Orders, in Brazil from 1549 to 1759 we see such a predominance of the Jesuits that the work of the other religious institutes is left somewhat obscured. This contrast was no more than the reflection of the situation in the respective home countries. . . . Of course, in Portugal the Mendicant Orders existed, and they exercised an important activity, but never did they develop to the same extent as in Spain. . . . Therefore, the expulsion of the Jesuits in 1759 had much graver consequences than the same expulsion from Spanish dominions eight years later, although this also was a very mistaken measure. The disappearance of the Society of Jesus created in Portugal and Brazil a vacuum which nothing could fill

---

[7] Esteban Fontana, "La expulsión de los jesuítas de Mendoza y sus repercusiones económicas," *Revista Chilena de Historia y Geografía*, No. 130 (1962), pp. 47-115. The *Juntas de Temporalidades* were local bodies set up for the administration of the confiscated Jesuit properties.

and gave to the Portuguese Church such a blow that she recuperated only with much difficulty and very slowly, whereas the Spanish Church resisted the wound much better, because of the importance and activity of the Mendicant Orders. This fact explains, together with other facts . . . the relative weakness of the Catholic tradition in Brazil, where the Church in my view is less powerful than in the majority of the Spanish-American republics.[8]

Ricard's statement leads us to another difficult question. What was the relative importance of the Jesuit Order in comparison with other religious bodies from the point of view of the Indian mission, colonial education, culture, and economy? A good and balanced assessment still remains to be done in the case of both regions, but both the partisans and foes of the Jesuits often seem to exaggerate the relative importance of the Jesuit contribution as a natural result of its controversial and highly publicized nature. One should, for example, not forget that they never carried out such an extensive mission in Spanish America as the Franciscans did before, during, and after their time. The Dominicans were perhaps their equals as scholars and teachers. The hierarchy was, as we have explained before, never recruited among the Jesuits, and the Inquisition also remained largely outside their influence.

To sum up, it may be maintained that scholarly and unbiased examinations of the entire complex of problems related to the expulsion of the Jesuit Order from the Spanish and Portuguese empires still remain to be made. The most satisfactory account of the complicated chain of events remains that given by Ludwig von Pastor but is scattered in different chapters of his gigantic *History of the Popes* and is obviously pro-Jesuit. It is also evident that recent advances within different fields of the historical discipline such as economic history and intellectual history offer

---

[8] His contribution in *Studies Presented at the Conference on the History of Religion in the New World During Colonial Times* (Washington, 1958), p. 113.

stimulating new approaches to the study of the Jesuit drama.

The reader of this little book is expected to realize what a multiplicity of factors were shaping events making it quite impossible to cover historical truth with simplistic generalizations. If so he does, the texts presented in the book may also serve as an introduction to research and as a stimulus for undertaking it.[9]

---

[9] So far as the selection of texts is concerned it should be kept in mind that many an interesting discussion or monographic treatment does not lend itself to presentation in the form of excerpts. If some aspects have been neglected in the selection it may also be because they have never been discussed in a more interesting and serious way.

I

The Jesuits and the Dawn

of a New Era

1

Salvador de Madariaga

THE FALL OF THE JESUITS— THE TRIUMPH OF THE PHILOSOPHERS

Born in 1886, Salvador de Madariaga, who began his career as an engineer, became deputy to the Cortes and Spanish Ambassador to the United States and France in the early 1930's. One of the outstanding intellectuals among the exiles after the Civil War of 1936-1939, Madariaga followed his second career, that of a university professor of Spanish studies at Oxford. By virtue of his great wit and literary talent—in both Spanish and English—Madariaga's many books on different subjects are widely read and admired. His historical interpretation of Spanish America as presented in his books on Columbus, Cortés, the Spanish Empire, and Bolívar is a very Hispanist one, only slightly modified by his liberal outlook. Many ultra-rightist historians would agree with him, however, when he ranks the Masons and the Jews as chief destroyers of the Spanish Empire. Madariaga also adds

Reprinted with permission of The Macmillan Company from *The Fall of the Spanish American Empire* (New York, 1948) by Salvador de Madariaga; excerpts from pp. 266-268, 274-280. Copyright 1947 by Salvador de Madariaga.

*the Jesuits to that list of mysterious "brotherhoods,"
but is evidently a little puzzled himself by the contradictions caused by this classification. Although a man
of extensive historical reading who usually thinks in
historical terms, Salvador de Madariaga can hardly be
considered a historian in the strict sense of the word.*

*After having characterized the Guaraní missions as
a "highly successful form of enlightened despotism
. . . in which the Indians were well treated, though
like children, and the interests of the Spanish state altogether disregarded," Madariaga continues:*

This very success was one of the causes of the downfall
of the Jesuits; but the chief reasons were of far wider
import. The campaign against them was the forerunner of
a war against the Catholic Church on the part of the "philosophers" and Encyclopedists. Hostilities would never have
broken out but for the philosophers, for the Society is
not warlike and the Jesuits had even tried to collaborate in
the famous Encyclopædia, writing the article on Theology. The leaders of this European movement were Voltaire and D'Alembert. . . .

Galling as it may be for its faithful, it is evident that by
then the Catholic Church stood not merely as the only,
but as the chief obstacle to intellectual progress. The authors of the Encyclopædia found that they had to submit
their texts to theological censors. Their scientific minds
found the claim not only irksome but extravagant. The
current of the human mind was flowing away from the
dogmatic Church which claimed the exclusive right to reg-
ulate it; and while it is questionable whether the direction in which it was moving was itself right, it was at any
rate relatively right when it demanded its freedom of error
as part of its movement toward truth. The Jesuits were not
attacked because they were the citadel of mental reaction,
which they were not; but because they were its scouts,
the most get-at-able of the powerful army of the Church.
In their ultimate aims, therefore, these philosophers,
D'Alembert, Voltaire, Choiseul, Aranda, Roda, whatever

we may think of their methods, were justified. Something had to be done and they chose their adversary well. . . .

In Spain the philosophers, notably Voltaire, had two powerful admirers and disciples: Aranda and the Duke of Huéscar, later Duke of Alba. "I hasten to impart news to you which cannot but be agreeable to you," D'Alembert wrote to Voltaire on May 14, 1773. "The Duke of Alba, one of the greatest lords of Spain, a man of much intelligence and who was ambassador in France under the name of Duke of Huéscar, has just sent me twenty *louis* for your statue. The letter he has written to me on the subject is full of the most agreeable things about you." . . . As for Aranda, we know from a letter written him by Voltaire that he supplied the lusty patriarch of Ferney with excellent Spanish wines, silk and china, to the old man's delight. Huéscar and Aranda were the leaders of the movement which culminated in the expulsion of the Jesuits.

But, as in the case of France, the movement, though led by a free thinking impulse which was a spiritual necessity of the times, took on curiously tortuous forms, and its leaders did not disdain to borrow weapons from their adversaries, including that superstition it was their aim to destroy. That the moral character of the Spanish Jesuits was high and their influence on national standards on the whole favorable, cannot be doubted, since we have it on the authority of no less a censor of the Catholic Church than Blanco White.[1] Yet they were expelled not by the people but by the upper classes, whose sons they educated. This fact surely reveals some inner failing of a grave character. Then, as now, the chief enemies of the Jesuits came out of their own colleges. The only man in the conspiracy who did not belong to the nobility was Roda, a lawyer who, for lack of parchments, had been refused a fellowship in one of the major colleges of Salamanca. It was said of him that, on his spectacles, there were painted on one eye a Jesuit and on the other a fellow of Salamanca. He

---

[1] A Protestant convert, the Spaniard Blanco White is known as the author of *Letters from Spain by Don Leucadio Doblado* (London, 1822) [ed.].

took power determined to destroy both the Jesuits and
the major colleges of Spain. He became Minister of Justice
under Charles III, and introduced a plan of educational
reform well inspired and progressive on its intellectual
side, lamentable from a wider point of view, for it destroyed the six colleges (four in Salamanca, one in Valladolid and one in Seville) which, purged of their abuses and
defects, might have maintained a valuable tradition of
scholarship and mental manners in the country.

This attitude was typical of the day: intellectualist, progressive, abstract and contemptuous of traditional values
which, under their dusty overgrowth, were biologically
sound. With Charles III, a well-meaning, good-hearted but
not intelligent monarch, this generation of men found their
opportunity. The King had lost touch with the country he
was to rule owing to a long residence abroad as Prince of
Parma and later King of Naples. The Jesuits, powerful in
the previous reign, lost their grip on the Court at the same
time as Ensenada, the Minister of Ferdinand VI, fell from
power; and as Charles III veered from a pro-English to a
pro-French policy, and the intimacy between the Bourbon
Courts developed into the Family Pact, the influence of the
"philosophic" Court of France was felt in Spain and its
methods imitated. The King had a confessor, Father Eleta,
known as Father Osma from the city in which he had
been born. There had been a Bishop of Osma in the previous
century, Palafox, famous for his quarrels with the Jesuits,
as Bishop of Puebla de los Angeles in New Spain. Roda
conceived the idea of attracting the powerful confessor to
his views by asking Rome to canonize Palafox, and the
spell worked. Better still, it revealed that the King himself
could be held by similar means. While still a young Infante,
as the third son of Philip V, King Charles had visited a
saintly lay brother in Seville, Brother Sebastian, who took
a fancy to him and predicted he would be King. At the
time, the prophecy was so far removed from probability
that, when it came true, the King was persuaded that the
lay brother had holy powers, and wanted him canonized.
Roda was delighted. The more the merrier. The Jesuits
would oppose the canonization of Palafox and trouble

could thus be expected for them in Spain. The King's most precious treasure was a manuscript prayer book given him by Brother Sebastian. He carried it in his pocket and laid it under his pillow at night. The Vatican claimed it as a piece of evidence. Every precaution was taken to convey it to Rome and back and everything prepared so that the King should be deprived of it for only the shortest possible time. While his amulet was away, Charles neither slept, nor ate, nor spoke, nor even hunted; he hardly breathed. And when he found that his heavy sacrifice had availed nothing, and that Rome procrastinated, his anger knew no bounds and the Jesuits were made the object of it.[2]

The Esquilache Riot came to clinch the matter. Esquilache (Squilacci) had been brought over from Naples by Charles as Minister of Finance. He was grasping, coarse and tactless, but well-meaning and progressive. He cleansed and improved the city, turned on hard the screw of taxation, and organized a monopoly of oil, bread and other staple foods which raised their price; he improved street-lighting in Madrid, where he installed 5,000 lamps, in order to check crime and vice at night; and with the same end in view prohibited wide-brimmed hats and flowing cloaks. The cloak is indispensable to the Spaniard, as two proverbs show: "Under a bad cloak there may hide a good drinker"; and "Under my cloak I kill the King." The Spaniard's cloak is the Englishman's castle. Madrid rose in revolt, on Easter Sunday, March 23, 1766, in a fury against the foreign Minister. *Viva el Rey, muera Esquilache* was the cry. Windows were broken and passers-by were made to unfold again the folded brims of their hats; but none was injured save some Flemish guards who barred the way to Esquilache's house to the crowd. The King in person came out on the balcony and made a verbal covenant with the people, promising to dismiss Esquilache and appoint a Spaniard, to cancel the Edict on hats and cloaks, to reduce the price of bread, oil and soap, to abolish all monop-

---

[2] This strange story Madariaga bases on an account given by Blanco White [ed.].

olies and to pardon the insurgents. A friar, crucifix in hand, read aloud the articles of the covenant, and the King beckoned "yes."

Then the unexpected happened. When all was calm, the King with his family and his Italian Minister left for Aranjuez in the still of night. Suspecting treachery, the crowd rose again next day. For forty-eight hours, a curiously well-controlled populace roared, shot volleys and blank musketry, barked furiously, hardly biting at all, and made much noise with little destruction. A coachmaker was sent to Aranjuez to demand the King's return. He brought back a written answer stating that the King had been bled twice, that Don Miguel Musquiz, a Spaniard, had been appointed Finance Minister, that the people were to disarm and go home and that nothing but obedience on the part of his subjects would induce the King to return to his capital. All went back to normal and the expenses and damage caused, mostly to public houses, were handsomely met. By whom? Who led this curious tumult? Who frightened the King into leaving his capital when all had been calm again? Who in fact started the whole affair? The answers seem today fairly clear. The Riot was a political bomb cleverly laid by the group of "philosophers" led by the Duke of Alba. "The calmness of the principal nobles at the moment when a general massacre was dreaded," the comings and goings, behind the crowd, of mysterious persons with a distinguished mien and self-possessed air; the ample funds and food the vociferous crowd never lacked; finally, the Duke of Alba's own deathbed confessions prove that the Riot was organized in order to frighten the King into expelling the Jesuits. Rumors that the Jesuits had been seen exciting the crowd, in particular one well-known Jesuit, Father Isidro López, circulated soon, and cries asking for the return of Ensenada were heard at the appropriate moment from the multitude.

The King was frightened. The disorders of Madrid had been echoed by similar scenes in Zaragoza, Cuenca, Palencia, Guipúzcoa, and it was assiduously put to him that the hidden hand of the Jesuits was behind it all. A secret inquiry set up by Roda led to no results, though it produced a crop of sentences of more than doubtful legal value;

. . . The most important political result of the whole affair was that Aranda became president of the Council of Castile and *de facto* dictator of Spain. He was ruthless and expeditive. Campomanes was entrusted with the "secret inquiry" on the events, and his first report explained that the rising had been due to "the evil ideas over the authority of the King spread by churchmen, and to the fanaticism which these churchmen had for many centuries instilled in the people and in simple folk." A "Special Court" or "Extraordinary Council" set up by Aranda, also under Campomanes, pointed straight at "the hand of a religious body which never ceases to inspire general aversion against the Government," and added that "it would be advisable to enlighten the people . . . and to disarm that dangerous body which everywhere tries to subjugate the throne and believes everything legitimate which allows it to reach its ends." On January 29, 1767, the Extraordinary Council presented its *Consulta*, in which after summing up all the grievances against the Jesuits, their expulsion was recommended "because the whole body is corrupted and all the fathers are terrible enemies of the peace of the Monarchy."

This report shows why absolute monarchies like France or Spain worked hand in hand with revolutionary philosophers against the Jesuits. Suárez, Mariana, Ravaillac and all that these names called forth must have weighed heavily on the mind of Charles III. He was told, moreover, that the Jesuits had engineered the riot of the preceding year; and that, as a number of (faked) letters "intercepted" and shown to him "proved," they had plotted to exterminate the royal family. One of these letters, supposed to have been written by Father Ricci, General of the Order, attributed to him the boast of having put together documents proving that Charles III was the son of Queen Isabel Farnese by Alberoni. At any rate, Charles made up his mind and Aranda was empowered to act on February 27, 1767. He worked in the utmost secrecy, children unable to understand being employed to copy documents. The same date was chosen for the whole of Spain—April second, though it was anticipated to March twenty-eighth in Madrid. The order was circulated under three seals. On the second envelope, the following words were written: "This packet is not to be opened till April 2, 1767, under pain of death." The order intimated full royal powers to arrest all the Jesuits and convey them as prisoners, in every case within twenty-four hours, to a port designated, where ships would wait; they were to be allowed to take away absolutely nothing but prayer books and linen for the crossing. Pain of death was threatened to the authorities concerned if one single Jesuit remained behind "even sick or dying."

On April second all residences of Jesuits were surrounded by troops and the *Pragmática* was published in which the King declared that "for reasons which he reserves to himself and following the impulses of his royal benignity, and making use of the supreme economic power which the Almighty had granted him for the protection of his vassals," he expelled the Jesuits; and he prohibited his subjects to write for or against his decision under pain of *lesa-Majestad*. A most typical decision of enlightened despotism. Progress by compulsion and no arguments allowed. "We have killed the son"—wrote Roda to Choiseul—"all that remains for us to do, is to do as much with the mother, our Holy Roman Church." In the Indies it was left to the discretion of the local authorities how and when to carry out the expulsion, but everything was done with similar precautions and silence. In New Spain it took place on June twenty-fifth. In several cities, notably San Luis Potosí, Guanajuato and Valladolid, the people rose in arms against the authorities and compelled them to receive the Jesuits back in their colleges. Armed forces had to be sent by the Viceroy, and more than 90 persons were executed before the Jesuits could be gathered in Veracruz and shipped to Genoa. In Buenos Aires and several other places the authorities had evidently feared similar events and did not carry out the order till they were sure of enough military backing. In Madrid the inhabitants of the capital were ignorant of the event till the following morning when the Jesuits and their escort were already far away on the road. It seems certain that more disorders might have taken place both in Spain and in the Indies had the Jesuits themselves decided to stand up to the law. But they obeyed everywhere.

2

Guillermo Furlong

THE JESUIT HERALDS OF DEMOCRACY AND THE NEW DESPOTISM

Early in this century, José Ingenieros, a well-known Argentine man of letters, summed up the liberal tradition by stating that the expulsion of the Jesuits had removed an obstacle for the Revolution of 1810. According to Ingenieros, the expulsion of 1767 gave rise to a division between liberales *and* jesuíticos *that was gradually transformed into the conflict between patriots and loyalists in 1810. Headed by the learned Jesuit Father Guillermo Furlong, a group of very Catholic, conservative, and nationalistic Argentine writers have in recent years advanced an interpretation which is the very opposite of that of Ingenieros. According to them, the "Jesuit doctrine" of society and government spelled democracy, thus provoking the action of royal absolutism in 1767. Consequently,*

Translated from *Presencia y sugestión del filósofo Francisco Suárez. Su influencia en la Revolución de Mayo* by Atilio Dell 'Oro Maini, Miguel A. Fiorito, and others (Buenos Aires, 1959); excerpts from pp. 81-86. Printed by permission of Guillermo Kraft Ltda. and of the author.

the Revolution of *1810* was in harmony with, and even theoretically based on, the Jesuit tradition.

Father Guillermo Furlong, born in 1889 and a Jesuit since 1903, is not essentially an advancer of daring hypotheses, however. He is, in the first place, a patient, most diligent scholar whose painstaking research has covered many aspects of the cultural and ecclesiastical history of the River Plate countries. Nobody knows more about the heterogeneous activities of the Jesuits in that area up to 1767/1768 than Father Furlong.

There was a general predominance of Suárez' doctrines in the middle of the eighteenth century. It was so great that on August 30, 1757, the Bishop of Asunción was able to write to Minister Wall that the Jesuits of the River Plate were in full control of every resource, stating: "The ecclesiastical prelates, the prebendaries and the priests are all theirs, for, it being generally believed here that the Jesuits are or have been the absolute sovereigns of the bishoprics, prebends, and parishes, all the others have tried to follow their school to such an extent that I have information of only one Thomist in this country, Doctor Leiva, the priest of Santa Fe. With the school of Saint Thomas being closed, a saying of Saint John is verified: *"Dilexerunt homines magis tenebras quam lucem"* (Men have preferred darkness to light).

When the Jesuits were expelled in 1767 an inventory was made of the books in their libraries, and in all of them copies of works on a wide range of subjects were found. In addition, the libraries of Santa Fe, Córdoba, Buenos Aires, Asunción, and Mendoza had abundant collections of the *Opera Omnia* by *Doctor Eximio* Francisco Suárez. Even nowadays there are many copies of Suárez' work carrying an *ex libris* dated before 1767, for example, the folio of *In tertiam partem Divi Thomae, tomus secundus*, which is kept in the library of the College of El Salvador (Buenos Aires) and which was at one time in the collection of the Society of Jesus in Córdoba.

There was nothing lacking in the so-called Great Library (Librería Grande) of the Principal College (Colegio

Mayor) and University of Córdoba, it being distinguished by that name from the other three libraries and collections which existed in the same institution and whose purposes were limited, thus restricting the number and content of their holdings. The Great Library had two remarkable commemorative displays. Above one of them could be seen an artistic sign reading: DR. ANG. STO THOMAS DE AQUINO, and this encompassed all the works of the great medieval thinker. Above the other could be read: DR. EX. P. FRANCISCO SUÁREZ, and here one could find the many works of the Spanish philosopher. There was a third display dedicated to the writings of Saint Ignacio de Loyola, patron of the University of Córdoba.

Before continuing in my exposition I am going to formulate an assertion which may be somewhat surprising. I have referred to the expulsion of the Jesuits in 1767, and I have dared to say that the effective cause of this act, the causes of which still intrigue historians, was nothing but the populist doctrine of Francisco Suárez. Very recently, although very timidly, Dr. Martínez Paz has indicated this cause. After recalling that, and they are his words, "the Jesuit doctrine, which came from Saint Thomas Aquinas or from Father Suárez, was without doubt rather favorable to democracy and hostile to the throne," he writes that "it occurs to us to think that the nature of this doctrine, between resistance and conspiracy, caused the expulsion [of the Jesuits] by the despotic government of Charles III."

That king showed himself very prudent by keeping in his royal breast the motives which had induced him to expel the Jesuits from all his dominions. He realized that those motives would have rebounded among the Americans with a perceptible prejudicing of the interests of the mother country. Had he expressed them frankly, he would have been forced to say: "I have expelled the Jesuits because there is no way to make them stop teaching, in their universities and colleges, doctrines which limit my royal prerogatives and put weapons in the hands of my subjects which may someday allow them to oppose me, their legitimate sovereign."

If Charles and his ministers did not express that fact with these words, their deeds certainly implied it. A few months after the collective expulsion of 1767, an abortive effort of impressing the Jesuit doctrines was made. This expulsion and suppression constituted one of the major and most tenacious royal preoccupations. A royal decree dated August 12, 1768, was directed to the Viceroys, Archbishops, et cetera, ordering that all the universities and schools should "destroy the Chairs of the School called Jesuit, and the authors of it should not be used for instruction"; but the undertaking was not easy. There were professors everywhere who were able to stop using the texts and books of the Jesuits, and who could even omit to mention the great masters of the Society of Jesus but who found it an impossible task, as it undoubtedly was, to deprive themselves of the doctrines which they themselves had assimilated while students and had taught so long. A second royal decree, dated October 18, 1769, again urged them to do so, establishing punishments for those who refused.

It was desired to eradicate in every way possible "the ideas and doctrines, corrupted in both the moral and political senses [note the expression *political sense*] divulged by the exiles and taught wherever they were authorized by the schools, colleges, and seminaries, and hardly any other Masters were recognized in all the Indies." Months later, on November 13, 1768, the battle was re-engaged with the goal of destroying the "unrest and turbulence which still existed as a result of the perverse suggestions of the seditious spirit of the exiles," and at the end of 1769[1] the substitution of sound doctrines for the lax and corrupt ones of the Jesuits was again urgently demanded. As Giménez Fernández has demonstrated amply and convincingly in his revelatory book *The Populist Doctrines in the Independence of Spanish America*, it was possible for the motherland to exile the Jesuits, but it was impossible to exile their doctrines, most especially those referring to the origins of the rights of kings.

About that which referred especially to the University of Córdoba, on June 7, 1768, the Count of Aranda wrote:

[1] "Months later" . . . refers to the decree of August 12, 1768. The text used here has "at the end of 1768," but a comparison with other accounts by Furlong shows that the year should be 1769 [ed.].

It is agreed that the university which Your Excellency suggests may be established in Córdoba of Tucumán, completely abolishing the doctrines of the exiled Jesuits and substituting those of Saint Augustine and Saint Thomas; placing there, by common assent of the Reverend Bishops, secular clergy of proven doctrine, and lacking them, regular priests for now, who may teach Theology, to the letter of Saint Thomas, the Cano *De Locis Theologicis,* and the moral theology of Natal Alejandro and of Daniel Concina, in order to purge laxity from moral opinions. The same thing is recommended to the Reverend Bishops and to the provincials of the Orders of Saint Dominic, Mercy, and Saint Francis, so that they may re-establish Christian morality and its purity, and with their priestly letters give notice of this to their respective diocese and subjects, in order that the faith and truth be maintained as is correct.

In the same document the Count of Aranda referred to the agreement to distribute the books from the Jesuit libraries among the universities and seminaries, and any remaining to the Dominican, Mercedarian, and Franciscan Fathers, "excepting those books dealing with the constitution and regime of the Society and any other papers dealing with these matters and their theological and moral authors, because those remain suspended until further notice."

That restless spirit of encyclopedic knowledge, Eusebio Llano Zapata, lived in Buenos Aires between 1751 and 1759. While his uncle, Monseignor Cayetano Marsellano y Agramont was bishop of that diocese, Llano Zapata wrote from Cádiz on January 9, 1767, six months before the expulsion of the Jesuits, and among other things he said the following to his correspondent, the Argentine Perfecto Salas:

I advise your Lordship to be very cautious with these priests [the Jesuits] and to be very restrained with them, although with a cheerful countenance and the fraternal love that charity inspires in us. Your Lordship should make certain that only the doctrine of Saint Thomas is followed in the seminary of Saint Toribio, and that it is attended by many university students from the colleges of the Dominican and Franciscan Fathers. Here, these schools are fashionable today, as they are of sound doctrine. Nobody should include in his curriculum vitae that he has studied with the Jesuits, in their schools or colleges. It is a dead party, and even damned.

This same Llano Zapata allows us to glimpse that which was malignant, odious, and condemned in the Jesuit doctrine by informing us, in another of his letters, that the scientific works of Mariana, Suárez, Busembaum, and other illustrious writers of the so-called Jesuit School had been consigned to the flames of the public bonfire by the hangman's hand in the capital of France, and that this was done "in order to contain doctrines which deal directly with the diminution of majesty." Mariana's book on the rights and duties of kings had been written for the instruction of the Austrians, and it was read and memorized unquestioningly by them. The very liberal Bourbons condemned this to the flames. And the tracts by Suárez on the democratic origin of authority, which had won the praise of the universities during the seventeenth and the first half of the eighteenth centuries, became the basic offender to the magnanimous sovereigns of the House of Bourbon.

What the concrete and precise Jesuit doctrine was that was being pursued with such tenacity was wisely kept secret from the general public. We will make it very clear further on,* but let us say for now that this was no other than that which made the people the primary depository of authority.

---

* In analyzing Suárez' thinking Furlong distinguishes four principles with regard to the origin and possession of power: (1) Nobody receives civil authority directly from God. (2) The governors receive their authority through intermediation of the people. (3) The people grants the authority by its free consent, and this is the source of the legitimate titles of power. (4) As a consequence of this transfer, the power becomes circumscribed both in the case of the governors who are the recipients of power and in the case of the people which grants it. While the former are not allowed to use this power arbitrarily, the latter should not resume it gratuitously [ed.].

3

Ricardo Krebs Wilckens

THE VICTIMS OF A
CONFLICT OF IDEAS

❖❖❖❖❖❖❖❖❖❖

*One of the principal actors in the dramatic course of
events that led to the expulsion of the Jesuits from the
realm of Charles III was Pedro Rodríguez, Count of
Campomanes (1723-1802), best known for his achievements as an economist. In 1762 he was appointed pros-
ecuting attorney (fiscal) to the Council of Castile, a
key position from which he helped to transform the
investigation of the Hat and Cloak Riots into a process
against the Jesuits. In a thoughtful study, the Chilean
historian Ricardo Krebs Wilckens (born in Valparaiso
in 1918; after studies in Germany a teacher at the Universidad de Chile since 1945) has recently set out to
analyze the vast historical, political, and economic
thinking of Campomanes. Although the importance of
Spanish regalist concepts in the downfall of the Jesuits
is rather obvious having, of course, been noticed before, this account by the Chilean student, written in
terms of the ideology of an outstanding Spanish intel-*

Translated from Ricardo Krebs Wilckens, *El pensamiento histórico, político y económico del Conde de Campomanes* (Santiago de Chile, 1960), excerpts from pp. 151-155. Printed with
the permission of the Comisión Central de Publicaciones de la
Universidad de Chile and of the author.

*lectual and bureaucrat of the time, is an unusually clear
and lucid one of this important aspect of the expulsion.*

C ampomanes was one of the principal promoters of the
expulsion of the Jesuits. His own explanations, which
coincide fundamentally with the arguments which were
officially given to justify the expulsion, are summarized in
the following passage:

The abuse of lax opinions and probabilism is the patri-
mony of the Society of Jesus. Within this organization
it is considered a sacrilege if any individual dares to
discuss the opinions of the Society and much less to
contradict them, having to respect as infallible oracles
the decisions made by the organization, which is the
only master of the opinions of its members. It would
not be convenient to give a lengthy account of probabilism, of philosophical sin, of idolatry, of perjury
with the title of mental restriction, of theft with the
pretext of compensation, of homicide with the pretext
of defense, and of regicide and tyrannicide with the
pretext of liberating the people from oppression. The
books [of the Jesuits] are full of sacrilegious opinions
on these points. The practice of this organization has
corresponded to its theory and there are various examples of revolutions promoted by it since its birth in
order to create confusion.

Hence Campomanes accuses the Jesuits of having taught
erroneous ideas and even of being heretics and of having
acted in seditious manner. What is the significance and
scope of these statements?

Campomanes' criticism refers, in the first place, to the
"Jesuit Doctrine," that is to say to probabilism, laxism, and
other theories sustained by the Jesuits or attributed to them,
and which being labeled by their enemies as false, heretical,
and dangerous, had given rise to violent discussions, and
had divided opinions in the universities. The expulsion
of the Society meant also the elimination of the "Jesuit
Doctrine." The government, basing itself on information

from the attorneys Campomanes and Floridablanca, agreed to suppress the professorships of the Jesuit school and to prohibit the use of the works of Jesuit authors in theological studies and ethics (Royal decrees of July 1, August 12, 1768; July 29, 1769).

Aside from their immediate consequences, these measures had wide repercussions and only reveal their entire significance when understood in relation to the great efforts Campomanes and his collaborators undertook to reform the university and Spanish intellectual life in general.

The estrangement of the Jesuits permitted the Crown to obtain control over the universities and the major colleges [Colegios Mayores] and to subject them to its will. Within the objective of assuring forever the triumph of regalism, the Crown—as we have mentioned before—ordered all faculty members to swear that "ultramontane" theories contrary to royal rights would not be taught. Royal censors were established in all universities to warrant the observance of this provision.

The triumph over the Jesuits and the "Jesuit Doctrine" meant at the same time a triumph over traditional education and in particular over scholasticism and Aristotelianism. As a consequence of the reforms promoted by Campomanes, the study of the following was introduced in the universities: the Scriptures, patristic tradition, history of the primitive Church and of the Councils, natural law, national law, national language, and the new critical methods in the historical as well as in the scientific disciplines. There was an increase in the reading of such foreign authors as Grotius, Pufendorf, Fleury, and Bossuet. The University of Zaragoza adopted as its text for canonical law the controversial work by Van Espen. Febronius' book began to circulate.

The aforementioned works and authors reveal the aims and the content of the reform of university education. This corresponded with the desire to incorporate into Spanish intellectual life the innovating tendencies of French ecclesiastical culture of the seventeenth and eighteenth centuries. The reform meant, of course, a reaction against some aspects of traditional Spanish culture, but it did not make a violent break with or oppose the religious and ecclesiastical culture in general. And it certainly did not mean a sellout to the atheistic and liberal tendencies of French encyclopædism.

The writings of Campomanes, as well as the reforms made in Spain as a consequence of the expulsion of the Jesuits, permit us to conclude that the suppression of the Society was partially the result of doctrinal causes. But one should not commit the error of interpreting this intellectual reaction against the Jesuits in the sense of a radical opposition against Christian religion and the Catholic Church. It was rather a matter of assimilating certain tendencies of Christian thought which were partly related to the primitive Church and biblical, apostolic, and patristic tradition, and partly born out of the contact with modern sciences. As a whole, it was French Gallicanism—mainly since the seventeenth century—which influenced this process. The Spanish reformers saw in the Jesuits the principal defenders of a tradition which they felt had become sterile, and they believed that the extinction of Jesuitism was an indispensable condition to rejuvenate intellectual life in Spain.*

The second accusation Campomanes made against the Society had a political character. His attacks against the "abominable and sacrilegious theories" and against the seditious intentions of the Jesuits must not be interpreted literally. In those days, the regulars of the Society were as devoted to the monarchy and as convinced of the king's divine rights as any other vassals of Charles III. Therefore, the regicide theory developed by Mariana, about 200 years before, lacked any basis even among the Jesuits themselves. It seems that the accusations that the Jesuits, acting seditiously, had been responsible for the mutiny of Esquilache cannot be sustained either.

The words of Campomanes in regard to the Jesuits' conspiracy against the monarchy must be interpreted in the wide sense of their unwillingness to submit to the nationalistic regalism and centralizing absolutism of Charles III.

---

* This identification of the Jesuits with the Latin-ecclesiastic tradition should not make us forget that there were "modern" Jesuits in the eighteenth century who adopted the new tendencies and tried to reform education. . . .

Campomanes saw in the Society a foreign body within the monarchy:

> Its system prescribed almost nothing more than that they reduce all rules known to mankind to such a point that they were totally subjugated to the Jesuits' use and direction. . . . They maintained that churchmen were not actually subjects of the kings, thus having the effect of creating two monarchies within the State, one temporal and one spiritual; this last one completely subject to the Curia.

Hence Campomanes saw in the Society a dangerous adversary to the absolute national monarchy. His accentuated regalism was in opposition to the international and ultramontane character of the Society. He felt that the Jesuits aspired to universal domination and the subordination to a single theocratic central power. The severe discipline of the regulars of the Society, and their unconditional obedience to the General and the Pope, seemed, to this zealous defender of national sovereignty and royal rights, a crime of lese majesty.

The will of Campomanes to conquer for the Crown the absolute sovereignty and to put at its disposal all the forces of the nation encountered the greatest obstacles in the religious communities where independence was protected by ample immunities and extensive properties. He bitterly complained that "the regulars tried by all means to extract themselves from the subjection to civil authority in all and for all," and that "the regulars do not hold themselves as vassals or subjects." The elevated number of priests took useful subjects from the State and the mortmain estates deprived it of economic strength. The privileges and exemptions of the religions reduced its political power.

Considering these facts, the kings of Spain had tried to obtain a certain influence over the Orders, being guided by a national point of view, as was clearly manifested by the policies of Philip II. These tendencies were accentuated by Charles III, who, in his "Reserved Instruction" stated that the "consent of the Roman Curia should be obtained so that all religious orders could be subjected to a discipline more in conformity with their institution and the State. Within the kingdom there should be a national superior who could closely supervise the discipline, be responsible for negligencies or relaxations, avoid losses and travel expenses to foreign countries in connection with chapters, and to have love and zeal for my service and the good of the fatherland."

Charles III expressed his satisfaction at having obliged the Roman Curia to name national superiors for the Trinitarians and the Carthusians, and lamented not having done the same with the orders of Saint Francis and Saint Augustine.

The monarch applied the same national criteria to the religious orders in the Indies.

But nationalist regalism proved impractical to the Society of Jesus. Even though the order had a marked Spanish character and was closely tied to Spanish history, because of its organization and general aims it had to refuse to submit totally to the sovereignty of the national state. The Society of Jesus was essentially ultramontane and curialist and constituted the principal representative and defender of papal theocracy. Because of this, the regalists saw in the Society their greatest adversary, one with which it seemed impossible to negotiate. This is how Campomanes expressed it at the Extraordinary Council of November 30, 1767: "Any faction within any state is incompatible with the subsistence and conservation of the state itself: in a way that, either the civil government must succumb and perish, or this deadly society must be expelled as a real political disease of the most acute kind ever known."

The expulsion of the Jesuits was not therefore the result of obscure machinations of certain conspirators, nor was it the work of enlightened rationalists and anticlericals who would have liked to deal a mortal blow to the Catholic religion, but rather it had its origin in the antagonism between ecclesiastical regalist nationalism and papal theocracy. From a more general viewpoint one can say that the Society of Jesus was a victim of the clash between the modern state which fought for its autonomy and complete sovereignty and the medieval and antireformist principle according to which the temporal must be subordinated directly to religious ends.

The Jesuits in the
New World

4

Robert Southey

THE GUARANÍ MISSIONS—
THE DESPOTIC WELFARE
STATE

*For late eighteenth-century writers the Jesuit state of
Paraguay was still mainly a political issue. Early nine-
teenth-century writers, however, under the influence
of romanticism, began to consider it a historic problem. A romantic figure of English letters, Robert
Southey (1774-1843), gradually moved in his political
opinion from the Jacobin left to the Tory right. When
he wrote his famous* History of Brazil *(1810-1819) he
was about halfway on that ideological itinerary. His
interest in Portuguese and Spanish subjects was awak-
ened by visits to the Iberian Peninsula. In Southey's
library of 14,000 volumes were many concerned with
Hispanic culture. Since he never visited South America himself, his writings on this part of the world were
entirely products of reading. Basing the account of
the "Jesuit State," included in his work on Brazil, on
the printed sources then available, his poetic intuition
enabled him to give it life. Southey is also famous as a*

From Robert Southey, *History of Brazil*, Vol. 2 (London, 1817),
excerpts from pp. 332-364.

master of English prose; the History of Brazil *is one of his best works.*

Here [in Paraguay] were innumerable tribes, addicted to the vices, prone to the superstitions, and subject to the accumulated miseries of the savage life; suffering wrongs from the Spaniards, and seeking vengeance in return; neither acknowledging King nor God; worshipping the Devil in this world, and condemned to him everlastingly in the next. These people the Jesuits undertook to reclaim with no other weapons than those of the Gospel, provided they might pursue their own plans, without the interference of any other power; and provided the Spaniards, over whose conduct they could have no control, were interdicted from coming among them. The Spanish Government, whose real concern for the salvation of the Indians within its extensive empire, however, erroneous in its direction, should be remembered as well as the enormities of its first conquest, granted these conditions; and the Jesuits were thus enabled to form establishments according to their own ideas of a perfect commonwealth, and to mould the human mind, till they made a community of men after their own heart. Equally impressed with horror for the state of savage man, and for the vices by which civilized society was every where infected, they endeavoured to reclaim the Indians from the one, and preserve them from the other by bringing them to that middle state wherein they might enjoy the greatest share of personal comforts, and be subject to the fewest spiritual dangers. For this purpose, as if they understood the words of Christ in their literal meaning, they sought to keep their converts always like little children in a state of pupillage. Their object was not to advance them in civilization, but to tame them to the utmost possible docility. Hereby they involved themselves in perpetual contradictions, of which their enemies did not fail to take advantage: for on one hand they argued with irresistible truth against the slave-traders, that the Indians ought to be regarded as human, rational, and immortal beings; and on the other they justified themselves for treating them as though they were incapable of self-conduct, by endeavouring to establish, that though they were human beings, having discourse of reason, and souls to be saved or lost, they were nevertheless of an inferior species. They did not venture thus broadly to assert a proposition which might well have been deemed heretical, but their conduct and their arguments unavoidably led to this conclusion.

Acting upon these views, they formed a Utopia of their own. The first object was to remove from their people all temptations which are not inherent in human nature; and by establishing as nearly as possible a community of goods, they excluded a large portion of the crimes and miseries which embitter the life of civilized man. For this they had the authority of sages and legislators: and if they could have found as fair a ground-work for the mythology of Popery in the scriptures as for this part of their institutions, the bible would not have been a prohibited book wherever the influence of the Jesuits extended. There was no difficulty in beginning upon this system in a wide and thinly-peopled country; men accustomed to the boundless liberty of the savage life would more readily perceive its obvious advantages, than they could be made to comprehend the more complicated relations of property, and the benefits of that inequality in society, of which the evils are apparent as well as numerous. The master of every family had a portion of land allotted him sufficient for its use, wherein he cultivated maize, mandubi, a species of potatoe, cotton, and whatever else he pleased; of this land, which was called *Abamba*, or the private possession, he was tenant as long as he was able to cultivate it; when he became too old for the labour, or in case of death, it was assigned to another occupier. Oxen for ploughing it were lent from the common stock. Two larger portions, called *Tupamba*, or God's possession, were cultivated for the community, one part being laid out in grain and pulse, another in cotton; here the inhabitants all contributed their share of work at stated times, and the produce was deposited in the common storehouse, for the food and clothing of the infirm and sick, widows, orphans, and children of both sexes. From these stores whatever was needed for the church, or for the public use, was purchased, and the Indians were supplied with seed, if, as it often happened, they had not been provident enough to lay it up for themselves: but they were required to return from their private harvest the same measure which they received. The public tribute also was discharged from this stock: this did not commence till the year 1649, when Philip IV, honouring them at the same time with the title of his most faithful vassals, and confirming their exemption from all other services, required an annual poll-tax of one *peso* of eight *reales* from all the males between the ages of twenty-two and fifty; that of all other Indian subjects was five *pesos*. There was an additional charge of an hundred *pesos* as a commutation for the tenths; but these payments produced little to the treasury; for as the kings of Spain allowed a salary of six hundred *pesos* to the two missionaries, and provided wine for the sacrament and oil for the lamps, which burnt day and night before the high altar, (both articles of exceeding cost, the latter coming from Europe, and the former either from thence or from Chili,) the balance upon an annual settlement of accounts was very trifling on either side. . . .

As in the Jesuits' system nothing was the result of fortuitous circumstances, but all had been preconceived and ordered, the towns were all built upon the same plan. The houses were placed on three sides of a large square. At first they were mere hovels: the frame-work was of stakes firmly set in the ground, and canes between them, well secured either with withs or thongs; these were then plastered with a mixture of mud, straw, and cow-dung. Shingles of a tree called the Caranday were found the best roofing; and a strong compost, which was water proof, was made of clay and bullock's blood. As the Reductions became more settled they improved in building; the houses were more solidly constructed, and covered with tiles. Still, by persons accustomed to the decencies of life, they would be deemed miserable habitations, . . . a single room of about twenty-four feet square being all, and the door serving at once to admit the light and let out the smoke. The houses were protected from sun and rain by wide porticos, which formed a covered walk. They were built in rows of six or seven each; these were at regular distances, two on each of three sides of the square; and as many parallel rows were placed behind them as the population of the place required.

The largest of the Guaraní Reductions contained eight thousand inhabitants, the smallest twelve hundred and fifty, . . . the average was about three thousand. On the fourth side of the square was the church, having on the right the Jesuit's house, and the public workshops, each inclosed in a quadrangle, and on the left a walled burial-ground; behind this range was a large garden; and on the left of the burial-ground, but separated from it, was the Widows'-house, built in a quadrangle. The enemies of the Jesuits, as well as their friends, agree in representing their churches as the largest and most splendid in that part of the world. . . . They had usually three naves, but some had five; and there were numerous windows, which were absolutely necessary; for though the church was always adorned with flowers, and sprinkled upon festivals with orange-flower and rose-water, neither these perfumes nor the incense could prevail over the odour of an unclean congregation. . . .

An Indian of the Reductions never knew, during his whole progress from the cradle to the grave, what it was to take thought for the morrow: all his duties were comprized in obedience. The strictest discipline soon becomes tolerable when it is certain and immutable; . . . that of the Jesuits extended to every thing, but it was neither capricious nor oppressive. The children were considered as belonging to the community; they lived with their parents, that the course of natural affection might not be interrupted; but their education was a public duty. Early in the morning the bell summoned them to church, where having prayed and been examined in the catechism, they heard mass; their breakfast was then given them at the Rector's from the public stores; after which they were led by an elder, who acted both as overseer and censor, to their daily occupations. From the earliest age the sexes were separated; they did not even enter the church by the same door, nor did woman or girl ever set foot within the Jesuit's house. The business of the young girls was to gather the cotton, and drive away birds from the field. The boys were employed in weeding, keeping the roads in order, and other tasks suited to their strength. They went to work with the music of flutes, and in procession, bearing a little image of St. Isidro the husbandman, the patron saint of Madrid . . . this idol was placed in a conspicuous situation while the boys were at work, and borne back with the same ceremony when the morning's task was over. In the afternoon they were again summoned to church, where they went through the rosary; they had then their dinner in the same manner as their breakfast, after which they returned home to assist their mothers, or amuse themselves during the remainder of the day. . . .

Equal care was taken to employ and to amuse the people; and for the latter purpose, a religion which consisted so much of externals afforded excellent means. It was soon discovered that the Indians possessed a remarkable aptitude for music. This talent was cultivated for the church-service, and brought to great perfection by the skill and assiduity of F. Juan Vaz: in his youth he is said to have been one of Charles the Fifth's musicians; but having given up all his property, and entered the Company, he applied the stores of his youthful art to this purpose, and died in the Reduction of Loretto, from the fatigues which in extreme old age he underwent in attending upon the neophytes during a pestilence. . . .

The system upon which the Reductions were founded and administered was confessedly suggested by that which Nobrega and Anchieta had pursued in Brazil; the persons who matured it, and gave it its perfect form in Paraguay, were Lorenzana, Montoya, and Diaz Taño. Never was there a more absolute despotism; but never has there existed any other society in which the welfare of the subjects, temporal and eternal, has been the sole object of the government: the governors, indeed, erred grossly in their standard of both; but, erroneous as they were, the sanctity of the end proposed, and the heroism and perseverance with which it was pursued, deserve the highest admiration. . . .

But if the Jesuits were placed in circumstances where even their superstition tended to purify and exalt the character, calling into action the benevolent as well as the heroic virtues, it was far otherwise with the Indians; they were kept by system in a state of moral inferiority. Whatever could make them good servants, and render them happy in servitude, was carefully taught them, but nothing beyond this, . . . nothing which could tend to political and intellectual emancipation. The enemies of the Company were thus provided with fair cause of accusation: why, they said, was no attempt made to elevate the Indians into free agents? why, if they were civilized, were they not rendered capable of enjoying the privileges of civilized men? If the system were to lead to nothing better, then had the Jesuits been labouring for no other end than to form an empire for themselves. This argument was distinct from all those which originated in the enmity of political or religious parties, and undoubtedly had its full weight in latter times. In vain did the Jesuits reply that these Indians were only fullgrown children, and that they knew not whether their obtuseness of intellect were a defect inherent in the race, or the consequence of savage life. Such an answer was no longer relevant when generations had grown up under their tuition: they dared not insist upon the first alternative, which would have been admitting all that the *Encomenderos* and slave-dealers desired; but if there were no original and radical inferiority in the race, then was the fault in that system upon which the Reductions were established. Why, it was asked, will not the Jesuits recruit themselves from these Indians who are born and bred among them, when it is so difficult to procure missionaries from Europe, so expensive to transport them, and impossible to obtain them in sufficient numbers? Why does not the Company, which in other countries had acted with right Christian indifference toward casts and colours, admit Guaranies into its bosom? The answer was, that their superiors had determined otherwise, . . . that things were well as they were; the object was accomplished; the Indians were brought to a state of Christian obedience, Christian virtue, and Christian happiness; their *summum bonum* was obtained; their welfare here and hereafter was secured. To those who look forward for that improvement of mankind, and that diminution of evil in the world, which human wisdom and divine religion both authorize us to expect, the reply will appear miserably insufficient: but the circumstances of the surrounding society into which it was proposed that these Indians should be incorporated, must be considered, and when the reader shall have that picture before him he will hold the Jesuits justified.

5

Blas Garay

THE GUARANÍ MISSIONS—
A RUTHLESS EXPLOITATION
OF THE INDIANS

*In their struggle against their versatile Jesuit rivals the
Paraguayan colonists were usually defeated. In the
historical discussion or polemics on the "Jesuit State"
the voice of their descendants has also been almost
drowned in the midst of all the learned contributions
of the Jesuit or pro-Jesuit scholars. One of the few
Paraguayans to write about the Jesuits with some re-
semblance of scholarly ambitions was Blas Garay,
who as a young diplomat in France and Spain in 1896
and 1897 did some research in the archives. His book*
El comunismo de las misiones *was also used as an introduction to a Spanish edition of a work of the seventeenth-century chronicler Father Nicolás del Techo.
Both introduction and edition have been harshly criticized by the Jesuit historian Pablo Hernández. Without a doubt, Garay as a historian, in spite of all his*

From *Historia de la Provincia del Paraguay de la Compañía de
Jesús* by Nicolás del Techo, Vol. 1 (Madrid, 1897); excerpts
from the prologue by Blas Garay, pp. xxxii-cx. Hernández' criticism in his introduction to *Declaración de la verdad* by José
Cardiel (Buenos Aires, 1900).

efforts, was an amateur. That certainly did not prevent him from expressing very definite judgments on the Jesuits, the traditional foes of his forefathers. A fiery young Paraguayan politician, journalist, and intellectual, Blas Garay's life span was cut short by a bullet.

We find two notably different periods of Jesuit history in Paraguay; first, the primitive, during which the Fathers laid the foundations of their future republic, running great risks although they were always protected by the force of arms; enduring all sorts of discomforts with no other compensation than the satisfaction of augmenting the Christian fold; seeking only spiritual goods, and never searching for advantages from which the neophytes could not obtain copious benefits. They were dedicated to the service of God and religion, unmoved by personal ambition. They were surrounded by popular affection because they respected the rights of outsiders, and because power had not yet made them arrogant. However, after a few years their behavior changed, and in direct ratio to their increased power. They who were at first unselfish and humble missionaries became the ambitious rulers of the towns who little by little shook off all the natural laws to which they should have been subject. They concerned themselves with accumulating material wealth to the detriment of their Christian and civilizing mission. They persecuted those who sought to end their abuses or tried to combat their influence. They mastered the wills of the governors and bishops, sometimes because the latter owed their positions to the Jesuits, then again, perhaps, because greed and the promise of rich profits converted them to devotees. And finally, they turned their republic into a vast collective society of production. Shielded by the great privileges they had been able to obtain, they ruined the province of Paraguay, to whose worthy inhabitants they owed recognition for so many ideas. . . .

The Jesuit organization was completely dependent on the equality the Fathers maintained among the Guaraní, an equality so absolute that it annihilated their individual initiative by depriving them of every impulse for emulation, every inducement that might move them to exert some energy. For the bad received the same portion as the good, the industrious the same as the lazy, the quick as the slow, the intelligent as the dim-witted; they were fed, dressed, and treated according to their needs, not their deeds, and no one could evade the completion of his appointed task. Those who exercised a little authority were obliged to be the most assiduous and punctual of all, so the others might learn from their example.

The women did the same work as the men; they could not avoid it by virtue of their sex, even if they were pregnant or nursing mothers. They helped the men plow, weed, and sow the earth, and then to gather in and store the crop. It is said that they celebrated only the major festivals. The provincials did attempt to relieve the neophytes from such continual labor, though with little success, and when they observed the pernicious fruits the mixing of the sexes bore, they tried to avoid that, too.

The Indians' work began at dawn and lasted until sunset, with only two hours of rest which were granted at noon for lunch.

. . . Agriculture was a principal source of wealth for the towns of the Jesuits. The lands employed in this were ultimately divided into three sections: the first, the *tabambaé*, belonged to the community; another, the *abambaé*, was reserved for the family heads, who each cultivated a portion as his own; the last, called *Tupambaé*, was the property of God.

All the mission Indians worked the first portion on the first three days of the week, under the strict inspection of wardens who were charged with ensuring that they applied themselves to the task diligently. The crops belonged to the community and were kept in the Society warehouses whence they were distributed as needed by the mission.

At first private property did not exist, even in name, and all the fruits of the Indians' labor were deposited in the communal granaries. The Jesuits had convinced the Court that the Guaraní were so improvident and ignorant that if the work was left to their direction they would not be able to maintain themselves. This argument did some violence to the truth, for as Azara well observes, one can hardly understand then how they managed to subsist and to multiply so prodigiously before the conquest, when they were still ignorant of the political and economic maxims of the Society; nor how other towns, founded by the Spaniards, could prosper. One also wonders how, outside Jesuit jurisdiction, the Indians could accept and protect private property, even though they had to serve the encomenderos.

After this system had endured for a great many years the Court, acceding to the insistent and authoritative requests it constantly received, told the Jesuits that it was high time the Indians learned both to govern themselves and to enjoy the advantages of owning their own property. Furthermore, they were informed that it seemed that the time for ending the communal regime had arrived. After exhausting every possible means of eluding the reform, the Fathers finally assigned, to quiet the objections and complaints, a certain plot of land to the head of each family, so that he and his family might cultivate and exploit it to their own advantage. Three days of the week were to be used for this, and the other three for the public benefit. Unfortunately the new arrangement did not produce the expected results. As every administrative notion had been lost, or was, rather, unknown to these unfortunates who had never had, nor imagined that they might have anything of their own, it could hardly be expected that, by luck, they should succeed in conforming to the exact amounts which they produced, thus avoiding misery and poverty. The missionaries knew this well; they relied on it in order to resist the innovation. "The Indians are incapable of governing themselves"; but they forgot to add that this incapacity was not native, but the result and fruit of deliberate education, of the complete isolation in which they lived, and of their removal from every occasion for learning anything inconvenient to the plans of the Fathers. The latter, on the other hand, made it difficult for the neophytes to work their own plots at the time allotted them by employing them overtime in the community service and the cultivation of the yerba maté. They also refused to pay them their just salaries, and obliged them to sell what they raised or made for themselves to the Society, at a loss. They refused them oxen for plowing, forcing them to pull the plows themselves, and hindered them in various other ways. Thus, the crops were either scanty or failed altogether. The Indians lacked what they needed for subsistence, and the community no longer assuaged their hunger. As that hunger pinched, and their scruples were scarce and accommodating, they sought from robbery what their work refused them, despoiling other unfortunates who were scarcely more comfortable or well supplied. Such evil tendencies triumphed over the most energetic and best-intentioned provisions of the provincials.

So that no one would avoid doing his share, the Jesuits found a method of handling the lazy ones, who showed no inclination to work, subjecting them to a particular regime. With this in mind the children and laggards were assigned to the *Tupambaé*, which were always on the best land in town, under the vigilance of special wardens who merited the Fathers' full trust and were charged with forcing them to fulfill the duties they were assigned, according to their ability, to the letter. The wardens denounced them for punishment, always severe and never excused, when they did not.

The crops from God's portion were also stored in the communal granaries and were to be used for the support of the old, ill, widows, chiefs, artisans, and those who were otherwise employed. This designation was only nominal and intended to impress the Indians, for actually, everything the missions produced had only one purpose; to advance the plans of the Society. Only a little was kept back to supply the needs of those who produced it by the sweat of their brows, and the continuous labor to which their catechists subjected them. Careless of their spiritual education, the Jesuits were careful only to train them as hardworking agriculturists or able artisans in those arts from which they might obtain the most profitable advantages. . . .

The culture of yerba maté also provided a useful resource, and the Jesuits had almost completely monopolized trade in it, being the only ones who sold the so-called *caaminí*, which was the most prized and expensive. As they had not undertaken this enterprise immediately and as it was notorious that it had cost the lives of thousands of Guaraní, they made early complaints which resulted in the

Indians being absolutely forbidden by law to be employed in its gathering. The complaints were positive and very reasonable. But were they inspired by charitable sentiments or angry rivalries? It is difficult to trust the Society's sincerity when one considers that, without changing any of the conditions inherent in the exploitation of yerba, they then set their neophytes to the work in spite of the fact that it had been forbidden as a result of their own efforts. . . .

Thus the Jesuits in Paraguay succeeded, not in converting all the souls they might have gained in such a populous region, but in becoming wealthy. Authoritative estimates are that the annual return of these missions was approximately one million Spanish silver pesos, and less than one hundred thousand was spent on their maintenance. Such copious profits allowed the Fathers to allay the increasing expenses of the Order in Europe generously, almost prodigiously, with the fruit of the Indians' labor. Their goal was the defense of their power structure, the eternal object of rude and obstinate attacks, made in passion sometimes, but more often in the spirit of justice.

The Jesuit solicitors, who were sent back to the old continent every six years, always bore respectable sums of money, and besides, there were the amounts sent to Rome very frequently by means of the English and Portuguese. In 1725, 400,000 pesos were sent in one single instance, and this is not necessarily the most splendid example of the Fathers' wealth. Such a sum does explain the success the Society always had in its negotiations, despite the fact that the rightness of its cause was frequently questionable.

This wealth, combined with the fear of being judged as enemies by a group so unscrupulous in its choice of means to an end, also explains the favour shown the Jesuits by most of the governors and bishops, who seemed their humble inferiors rather than their superiors. . . .

6

Robert Cunninghame Graham

THE GUARANÍ MISSIONS—
A VANISHED ARCADIA

◇◇◇◇◇◇◇◇◇◇◇◇

*While French and German writers have often chosen
the "Jesuit State" as the starting point for the construction of social theories and endless speculation, the
theme has exercised much less appeal on the Anglo-
Saxon mind. One of the few monographs on the subject is* A Vanished Arcadia *by Robert Cunninghame
Graham (1852-1936), known as one of the founders of
the British Labour Party, as a Scottish nationalist
leader, and as the author of many biographies and
travelogues, most of them dealing with Latin America. In his foreword, signed in 1900, the author states
that his "only interest in the matter is how the Jesuits'
rule acted upon the Indians themselves, and if it made
them happy"—more happy or less happy than the Indians administered directly by the authorities or subjected to the* encomienda *system. To find the answer,
Cunninghame Graham did much reading, including
that of some documents in Spanish archives, and he
also rambled over the grounds where the Guaraní*

From *A Vanished Arcadia: Being Some Account of the Jesuits
in Paraguay, 1607 to 1767*, by R. B. Cunninghame Graham (New
York: The Dial Press, 1924), excerpts from pp. 196-212.

missions once prospered. His ideas about Spanish-American legislation and social reality were somewhat vague, however, and he did not care to distinguish between chattel slaves and encomienda Indians. Consequently, for Cunninghame Graham there was no alternative to the "Jesuit State" other than slavery.

M uch has been written of the interior government of the missions by the Jesuits, but chiefly by strong partisans, for and against, on either side, whose only object was to make out a case to fit the prejudices of those for whom they wrote. Upon the Jesuit side the Abbé Muratori describes a paradise. A very Carlo Dolce amongst writers, with him all in the missions is so cloying sweet that one's soul sickens, and one longs in his "Happy Christianity" to find a drop of gall. For full five hundred pages nothing is amiss; the men of Belial persecute the Jesuit saints, who always (after the fashion of their Order and mankind) turn both cheeks to the smiter, and if their purse is taken, hasten to give up their cloaks. The Indians are all love and gratitude. No need in the Abbé's pages for the twelve pair of fetters which Brabo most unkindly has set down among his inventories. . . . Then comes Ibañez, the ex-Jesuit, on the other side. In a twinkling of an eye the scene is changed. For, quite in Hogarth's vein, he paints the missions as a perpetual march to Finchley, and tells us that the Indians were savages, and quite unchanged in all their primitive propensities under the Jesuit rule. For the Jesuits themselves he has a few home truths administered with vinegar, after the fashion of the renegade the whole world over, who sees nothing good in the society that has turned him out. He roundly says that the Jesuits were loafers, accuses them of keeping the Indians ignorant for their own purposes, and paints them quite as black as the Abbé Muratori painted them rose-colour, and with as little art. So that, as usually happens in the writings of all polemics, no matter upon which side they may write, there is but little information, and that distorted to an incredible degree, is all that they afford.

In general, curious as it may appear, the bitterest opponents of the Jesuits were Catholics, and Protestants have often written as apologists. Buffon, Raynal, and Montesquieu, with Voltaire, Robertson, and Southey, have written favorably of the internal government of the missions and the effect which it produced. No other names of equal authority can be quoted on the other side; but yet the fact remains that the Jesuits in Paraguay were exposed to constant calumny from the first day they went there till the last member of the Order left the land.

It is my object first to try to show what the conditions of their government really were, and then to try and clear up what was the cause of unpopularity, and why so many and such persistent calumnies were laid to their account. Stretching right up and down the banks of both the Paraná and Uruguay, the missions extended from Nuestra Señora de Fé (or Santa Maria), in Paraguay, to San Miguel, in what is now the Brazilian province of Rio Grande do Sul; and from the mission of Corpus, on the east bank of the Paraná, to Yapeyú, upon the Uruguay. The official capital was placed at La Candelaria, on the east bank of the Paraná. In that town the Superior of the missions had his official residence, and from thence he ruled the whole territory, having not only the ecclesiastical but the temporal power, the latter, from the position in which he was placed, so many hundred miles from any Spanish governor, having by degrees gradually come into his hands. The little town of La Candelaria was, when I knew it, in a most neglected state. The buildings of the Jesuits, with the exception of the church, were all in ruins. The streets were sandy and deserted, the foot-walk separated from them by a line of hardwood posts which, as tradition said, were left there by the Jesuits. . . .

In every mission two chosen Jesuits lived. The elder, selected for his experience of the country and knowledge of the tongue, . . . was vested with the civil power, and was responsible directly to the Superior. The second, generally styled companion (*el Compañero*), acted as his lieutenant, and had full charge of all things spiritual; so that they were a check on one another, and their duties did not clash.

In difficulties the Superior transmitted orders, like a general in the field, by mounted messengers, who frequently rode a hundred miles a day, relays of horses always being kept ready for emergencies every three leagues upon the road. From La Candelaria roads branched off to every portion of the territory, most of them fit for carts, and all superior to those tracks which were the only thoroughfares but twenty years ago. . . . In the districts of the Upper Uruguay and Paraná, besides the roads and relays of post-horses, they had a fleet both of canoes and boats in which they carried yerba and the other products of the land. Thus, with their fleet of boats and of canoes, their high-roads branching out on every side, and their relays of post-horses at intervals, probably no state of America at the time had such interior means of communication with the seat of government. . . .

The system of interior government in the missions was in appearance democratic—that is to say, there were officials, as mayors and councillors; but most of them were named by the Jesuits, and all of them, even although elected, owed their election entirely to their priests. This sort of thought-suggested representation was the most fitting for the Indians at the time, and those who look into the workings of a county council of today cannot but think at times that the majority of the councillors would have been better chosen had the electorate had the benefit of some controlling hand, though from what quarter it is difficult to see. The problem which most writers on the Jesuits have quite misunderstood is how two Jesuits were able to keep a mission of several thousand Indians in order, and to rule supreme without armed forces or any means of making their power felt or of enforcing obedience to their decrees. Undoubtedly, the dangerous position in which the Indians stood, exposed on one side to the Paulistas and on the other to the Spanish settlers, both of whom wished to take them as their slaves, placed power in the Jesuits' hands: for the Indians clearly perceived that the Jesuits alone stood between them and instant slavery. Most controversialists who have opposed the Jesuits assert that the Indians of the missions were, in reality, half slaves. Nothing is further from the truth, if one consults the contemporary records, and remembers the small number of the Jesuits. The work the Indians did was inconsiderable, and under such conditions as to deprive it of much of the toilsomeness which is incident to any kind of work. The very essence of a slave's estate is being obliged to work without remuneration for another man. Nothing was farther from the Indians than such a state of things. Their work was done for the community, and though the Jesuits, without doubt, had the full disposition of all the money earned in commerce and of the distribution of the goods, neither the money nor the goods were used for self-aggrandisement, but were laid out for the benefit of the community at large. The total population of the thirty towns is variously estimated at from one hundred and forty to one hundred and eighty thousand, and, curiously enough, it remained almost at the same figure during the whole period of the Jesuit rule.[1] This fact has been adduced against the Jesuits, and it has been said that they could not have been good rulers, or the population must have increased; but those who say so forget that the Indians of Paraguay were never in great numbers, and that most writers on the wild tribes, as Dobrizhoffer and Azara, remark their tendency never to increase.

All this relatively large population of Indians was ruled, as has been seen, by a quite inconsiderable number of priests, who, not disposing of any European force, and being almost always on bad terms with the Spanish settlers in Paraguay on account of the firm stand they made against the enslaving of the Indians, had no means of coercion at their command. Hence the Indians must have been contented with their rule, for if they had not been so the Jesuits possessed no power to stop them from returning to their savage life. . . .

Though it has been stated by many polemical writers, such as Ibañez and Azara, and more recently by Washburne, who was American Minister in Paraguay during the war with Brazil and the Argentine Republic (1866-70), that the Jesuits had amassed great wealth in Paraguay, no proof

---

[1] On the contrary, the statistics published by P. Hernández, *Organización social de las doctrinas guaraníes* . . . , II (Barcelona, 1913), 618, show considerable fluctuations [ed.].

has ever been advanced of such a charge. Certainly Cárdenas[2] made the same statement, but it was never in his power to bring any confirmation of what he said. This power alone was in the hands of Bucareli (1767), the Viceroy[3] of Buenos Aires, under whose auspices the expulsion of the Jesuits was carried out. By several extracts from Brabo's inventories, and by the statement of the receivers sent by Bucareli, I hope to show that there was no great wealth at any time in the mission territory, and that the income was expended in the territory itself. It may be that the expenditure on churches was excessive, and also that the money laid out on religious ceremonies was not productive; but the Jesuits, strange as it may appear, did not conduct the missions after the fashion of a business concern, but rather as the rulers of some Utopia—those foolish beings who think happiness is preferable to wealth. . . .

What was it, then, which raised the Jesuits up so many and so powerful enemies in Paraguay, when in the districts of the Moxos and the Chiquitos where their power was to the full as great, among the Indians, they never had a quarrel with the Spaniards till the day they were expelled? Many and various causes contributed to all they underwent, but most undoubtedly two reasons must have brought about their fall.

Since the time of Cárdenas, the report that the Jesuits had rich mines, which they worked on the sly, had been persistently on the increase. Although disproved a thousand times, it still remained; even today, in spite of "science" and its wonderful discoveries, there are many in Paraguay who cherish dreams of discovering Jesuit mines. Humanity loves to deceive itself, although there are plenty ready to deceive it; and if men can both forge for themselves fables and at the same time damage their neighbours in so doing, their pleasure is intense. I take it that many really believed the stories of the mines, being unable to credit that anyone would live far from the world, surrounded but by Indians,

---

[2] Bishop Bernardino de Cárdenas (1579-1668), famous because of his quarrel with the Jesuits in Paraguay [ed.].

[3] Francisco de Paula Bucareli was appointed governor of Buenos Aires in 1765. The first viceroy of Río de la Plata was appointed eleven years later [ed.].

for any other reason than to enrich themselves. So that it would appear one of the reasons which induced hatred against the Jesuits was the idea that they had enormous mineral wealth, which either they did not work or else worked in secret for the benefit of their society.

The other reason was the question of slavery. Once get it well into your head that you and yours are "reasoning men" (*gente de razón*), and that all coloured people are irrational, and slavery follows as a natural sequence; for "reasoning men" have wit to make a gun, and on the gun all reason takes its stand. From the first instant of their arrival in America, the Jesuits had maintained a firm front against the enslavement of the Indians. They may have had their faults in Europe, and in the cities of America; but where they came in contact with the Indians in the wilds theirs was the one protecting hand. . . .

On many occasions, notably in the time of Cárdenas, the Jesuits openly withstood all slavery, and among the concessions that Ruiz Montoya obtained from the King of Spain was one declaring all the Indians to be free. If more examples of the hatred that their attitude on slavery called forth were wanting, it is to be remembered that in 1640, when Montoya and Taño returned from Spain and affixed the edict of the Pope on the church doors in Piritinanga, threatening with excommunication all slave-holders, a cry of robbery went forth, and the Jesuits were banished from the town.[4] In this matter of slavery there is no saying what view any one given man will take upon it when he finds himself in such a country as America was during the time the Jesuits were in Paraguay. Don Felix de Azara, a liberal and a philosopher, a man of science, and who has left us perhaps the best description both of Paraguay and of the River Plate written in the eighteenth century, yet was a partisan of slavery. In a most curious passage for a liberal philosopher, he says: "The Court ordered Don Francisco,[5] Judge of the High Court of Charcas, to go to Peru in the character of visitor. The first measure which he took, in

---

[4] Only Francisco Díaz Taño, not Antonio Ruiz de Montoya, returned via Brazil [ed.].

[5] Should be Francisco de Alfaro [ed.].

1612, was to order that in future no one should go to the Indians' houses with the pretext of reducing them [i.e., to civilization], and that no *encomiendas* [fiefs] should be given of the kind we have explained—that is to say, with personal service [of the Indians]. I cannot understand on what he could have founded a measure so politically absurd; but as that judge favoured the *ideas of the Jesuits,* it is suspected that they dictated his conduct." [6]

What stronger testimony (coming from such a man) could possibly be found, both that the Jesuits were opposed to the enslaving of the Indians and that their opposition rendered them unpopular? In the same way, no doubt, some modern, unwise philosopher, writing in Brussels, would uphold the slavery and massacres in Belgian Africa as evidences of a wise policy, because the end condones the means, and in the future, when progress has had time to fructify, there will be workhouses dotted all up and down the Congo, and every "native" will be forced to supply himself, at but a trifle above the cost in Belgium, with a sufficiency of comfortable and thoroughly well-seasoned wooden shoes.

So it appears that the aforesaid were the two chief reasons which made the Jesuits unpopular with the Spanish settlers in Paraguay. But in addition it should be remembered that there were in that country members of almost all the other religious Orders, and that, as nearly every one of them had quarrelled with the Jesuits in Europe, or at best were jealous of their power, the enmities begun in Europe were transmitted to the New World, and constantly fanned by reports of the quarrels which went on between the various Orders all through Europe, and especially in Rome.

If it were the case that the Jesuits excited feelings of hatred in their neighbours, yet they certainly had the gift of attaching to themselves the Indians' hearts. No institution, condemned with contumely and thrust out of a country where it had worked for long, its supposed crimes kept

---

[6] See M. Mörner, *The Political and Economic Activities of the Jesuits in the La Plata Region . . .* (Stockholm, 1953), pp. 67, 82 [ed.].

secret, and its members all condemned unheard, could have preserved its popularity amongst the descendants of the men with whom it worked, after more than one hundred years have passed, had this not been the case.

I care not in the least for theories, for this or that dogma of politicians or theologists, but take my stand on what I heard myself during my visits to the now-ruined Jesuit missions in Paraguay. Horsemen say horses can go in any shape, and, wonderful as it may seem, men can be happy under conditions which no writer on political economy would recognize as fit for human beings. Not once but many times have aged Indians told me of what their fathers used to say about the Jesuits, and they themselves always spoke of them with respect and kindness, and endeavoured to keep up to the best of their ability all the traditions of the Church ceremonies and hours of prayer which the Jesuits had instilled.

That the interior system of their government was perfect, or such as would be suitable for men called "civilized" today, is not the case. That it was not only suitable, but perhaps the best that under all circumstances could have been devised for Indian tribes two hundred years ago, and then but just emerged from seminomadism, is, I think, clear, when one remembers in what a state of misery and despair the Indians of the *encomiendas* and the *mitas* passed their lives. That semicommunism, with a controlling hand in administrative affairs, produced many superior men, or such as rise to the top in modern times, I do not think; but, then, who are the men, and by the exercise of what kind of virtues do they rise in the societies of modern times? The Jesuits' aim was to make the great bulk of the Indians under their control contented, and that they gained their end the complaints against them by the surrounding population of slave-holders and hunters after slaves go far to prove.

Leaving upon one side their system of administration, and discounting their unalterable perseverance, there were two things on which the Jesuits appealed to the Indians; and those two things, by the very nature of their knowledge of mankind, they knew appealed as much to the Indians as to any other race of men. Firstly (and in this writers opposed to them, as Brabo and Azara, both agree), they instilled into the Indians that the land on which they lived, with missions, churches, herds, flocks, and the rest, was their own property. And in the second place they told them they were free, and that they had the King of Spain's own edict in confirmation of their freedom, so that they never could be slaves. Neither of these two propositions commends itself to many writers on the Jesuits in Paraguay; but for all that it seems to me that in themselves they were sufficient to account for the firm hold the Jesuits had on their neophytes.

The freedom which the Indians enjoyed under the Jesuit rule might not have seemed excessive to modern minds and those attuned to the philanthropic rule of the Europeans of today in Africa. Such as it was, it seemed sufficient to the Guaraní, and even, in a limited degree, placed them above the Indians of the Spanish settlements, who for the most part passed their lives in slavery.

7

Herbert E. Bolton

THE JESUITS—HEROES OF A MOVING FRONTIER

◆◇◆◇◆◇◆◇◆◇◆

*Few American historians have been more active in
molding opinion than Herbert Bolton (1870-1953),
the father of the Greater America theory and one of
the pioneers of Hispanic-American studies in the
United States. He was a professor at the University
of California at Berkeley from 1911 to 1940, and
was also director of its famous Bancroft Library. Bolton's outlook was determined by his contact with the
historical heritage of the American West Coast. The
first Spanish expeditions to California and the activities of Father Kino in present Sonora, Arizona, and
the Spanish borderlands provided him with the subjects
for his best-known works. Under these circumstances
his stress on the border function of the missions was
natural. The text offered here is taken from a speech
before the American Catholic Association in 1934, and
retains a certain rhetorical touch. It shows how the
Jesuits in Bolton's eyes were, above all, torchbearers
of Western civilization who penetrated a gigantic*

"The Black Robes of New Spain," from *Wider Horizons of
American History* by Herbert E. Bolton. Copyright, 1939, D.
Appleton-Century Company, Inc. Excerpts from pp. 149-188.
Reprinted by permission of the publisher.

wilderness with which the author seems to have been unusually familiar.

No phase of Western Hemisphere history reveals greater heroism, and few have greater significance, than that of the Jesuit missions. The story of the Black Robes in Paraguay and other parts of South America has been told by many writers. The deeds of the Jesuits in New France have been made widely known to English readers by the scintillating pages of Parkman, the monumental documentary collection edited by Thwaites, and the scholarly monographs of Kellogg and a host of Canadian scholars. . . .

But the Black Robes of New France were by no means the only sons of Loyola in the North American colonies. Indeed, they were not the earliest or the largest group, for they were long preceded and greatly outnumbered by those of New Spain. . . .

For nearly a score of years [after the arrival of the Jesuits in New Spain in 1572] effort was directed mainly toward establishing educational institutions, for which the young Order was already famous. Four colleges and a seminary were followed by the great Colegio Máximo of San Pedro y San Pablo, which received its papal charter sixty years before Harvard opened its doors, and soon took its place as one of the three or four leading universities in all America. . . .

Their maiden effort in missions *entre infieles* was at San Luís de la Paz, where they were sent to help tame the wild Chichimecos, those people who terrorized the highway leading from the capital to the mines of Zacatecas. Under the gentle influence of the Black Robes roving Indians turned to village life, warriors became farmers, and the roads were made safe. Spaniards settled in the vicinity, and the present city of San Luís de la Paz is the result. Thus the first Jesuit mission among the wild Indians of Mexico was typical of all: it became the nucleus of a Christian colony and a center of civilization.

The Chichimec mission was but a step toward the great heathendom of Nueva Vizcaya, that immense jurisdiction

embracing all the country beyond Zacatecas, and extend-
ing a thousand miles or more, to New Mexico and California. . . . Jesuit Land, for such the Northwest might well
be called, comprised the modern districts of Nayarit, the
four great states of Durango, Chihuahua, Sinaloa, and
Sonora, Baja California, and part of Arizona, a domain
larger than all of France. And the Black Robes did not
merely explore this vast area, they occupied it in detail.
This extensive region was chiefly a mountain country.
. . . The Indians of this vast expanse were of various lin-
guistic stocks and of many tribes. They occupied fairly
definite areas, but with a few exceptions they did not lead
a wholly sedentary life. For food most of the mainland peoples within the area raised maize, beans, and calabashes by
primitive methods; the Peninsula Indians practiced no agriculture at all. The natives of the mainland coast and the
foothills were the most numerous, the most docile, and offered the best missionary field.

The pioneer missionaries in Nueva Vizcaya were the
Franciscans. But the sons of Loyola now entered the district (1591), and became almost its sole evangelists during
the next century and three quarters. Then the Franciscans
came back. In two wide-fronted columns the Jesuits
marched northward up the mainland, one up the eastern
and one up the western slope of the imponderable Sierra
Madre, meeting generally west of the Continental Divide.
At the end of the seventeenth century they crossed the
Gulf and moved in a third phalanx into the Peninsula of
California.

River by river, valley by valley, canyon by canyon, tribe
by tribe, these harbingers of Christian civilization advanced
into the realm of heathendom. They gathered the natives
into villages, indoctrinated them in the Faith, trained them
in agriculture and the simpler crafts, and in schools and
seminaries taught many of them reading, writing, and music. Under the tutelage of the patient Jesuits, barbarians
who formerly had constructed only the meanest huts now
built substantial Christian temples, some of which still
stand as architectural monuments. The natives were generally well disposed toward the missionaries. But secular
Spaniards exploited their labor in mines and on haciendas;

and native priests were jealous of their white competitors. The result was a series of periodic Indian revolts in which a score or more of Black Robes in New Spain won the crown of martyrdom. But the march went on.

It was a colorful pageant. Black Robes moved into the wilderness beside or ahead of prospector, miner, soldier, cattleman, and frontier trader. Land travel was chiefly on horseback, muleback, or on foot, and land transportation by pack train or Indian carriers. As the frontier expanded, here and there a town, a mining camp, an hacienda, a garrison was pitched on the border of settlement. Still beyond, in the midst of heathendom, Christian missions were planted. As the Spaniards advanced northward, the Indians were reduced to sedentary life or were driven back. The spread of European civilization in North America was not by any means wholly a westward movement. . . .

The central feature of the mission was the pueblo, or permanent Indian village. The Black Robe went into the wilds seeking out heathen, making them his friends, telling them the Gospel story, baptizing the children of such parents as were willing, and adults who were dangerously ill. But this did not suffice. In order properly to indoctrinate the whole body of natives, drill them in the rudiments of Christian civilization, and give them economic stability, they were assembled in pueblos, or towns, organized to achieve these aims. If the natives already lived in a permanent and compact village, there the mission was established. There the work of "reduction" had already been done. With the wilder tribes pueblo-forming was often a difficult task, for they preferred to live in freedom in caves or huts. The mountain Tarahumares especially opposed reduction to pueblo life. As a nucleus of a new pueblo, it was the practice to bring a few families of Christianized Indians from an older mission, to help tame and domesticate the raw recruits. Customarily each Jesuit missionary had charge of three pueblos, a *cabecera*, and two *visitas*.

The heart of the mission and the pride of the padre was the church. Nearby was the residence of the pastor. Close at hand, perhaps in another quadrangle, were the houses of the Indians which constituted the pueblo. In a fully developed mission there were carpenter shops, blacksmith shops, spinning and weaving rooms, corrals for the stock, fields, irrigation ditches, and everything going to make a well-ordered and self-supporting agricultural unit. All this was supervised by the missionary himself, assisted sometimes by a lay brother expert in the mysteries of farm and forge. . . .

[About 1680] the Black Robes had established Christianity in the Sierra Madre and on both its slopes all the way from Southern Durango to northern Chihuahua, and from Culiacán to the Arizona border. On the northeast they were blocked by the Apaches as by a Chinese wall. But the way was open to the west and northwest, in Lower California and in Pimería Alta, where large and friendly populations lay still beyond the rim of Christendom. To cultivate these extensive vineyards now came Kino, Campos, Salvatierra, Ugarte, and a valiant host of only slightly less notable figures. Conspicuous among them all was Kino, Apostle to Pimería Alta. He arrived there in March 1687, the very month when La Salle met his tragic death in the wilds of Texas. He was just well started when the Pimas destroyed several missions and martyred Father Saeta at Caborca. But for a quarter-century he kept on. He personally baptized more than 4,500 Indians. His mission farms and ranches became the most prosperous in all Sonora. His demonstration that Lower California was a peninsula, not an island, reversed stubborn opinion. Of Pimería Alta he was not only the Apostle, but also explorer, ethnologist, cartographer, defender, cattle king, and historian.

With his dream of converting Lower California, Father Kino infected Salvatierra, who translated the vision into reality. The peninsula was assigned to the Jesuits on condition that they finance it themselves. In return they were made practically autonomous, like their brethren in Paraguay. Aided by the giant athlete Ugarte, Salvatierra raised and organized the celebrated Pious Fund, which is still in existence. Thus financed, he maintained a little fleet of transports which plied back and forth across the Gulf, carrying livestock and other supplies for barren Lower California, obtained chiefly from the mainland Black Robes. By the time of his death he and his associates had founded seven flourishing missions among almost-savage

Indians, on a rocky tongue of land scarcely capable of sustaining civilized life.

Ugarte now carried the Cross to the hostile people on the lower end of the peninsula, where the names of Carranco and Tamaral were added to the already long list of Jesuit martyrs. In the midcentury new foundations were made in the north, until nearly a score of successful missions were in operation, and many thousand Indians were settled in pueblo life. During their stay of seventy years in Lower California, more than fifty Black Robes, all told, labored in exile on this barren cactus patch.

The last three Lower California missions were made possible by a Borgian heiress. The tale is told that when she made the gift she was asked in what country she wished the missions established. "In the most outlandish place in the world," she replied. The Jesuits consulted their atlases and returned the answer: "The most outlandish place in all the world is California." So there the new missions were planted. . . .

A large missionary province, the result of many years of development, was like a tree. The fresh growth was near the top. So it was with the Province of New Spain. The roots of the plant were the central organization in Europe and Mexico. The colleges and other permanent foundations at the principal centers on the way north represented the trunk. As time went on, this trunk gradually became bare of missionary verdure. Between Durango and Pimería Alta in the eighteenth century there were missions in all stages of evolution, some already secularized, others old and stable, but without new blood from heathendom; still others, on the periphery, filled with the vigor characteristic of youth.

The Jesuits had always labored under a degree of insecurity due to causes other than Indian revolts. Frequently there was pressure for secularizing the missions, a step which was contemplated in the system. This pressure came from bishops for various reasons, from the government which wished to collect tribute, or from secular neighbors who were greedy for Indian lands or the right to exploit Indian labor. In the middle eighteenth century the missions among the Tepehuanes and in Tarahumara Baja were thus turned over to the parish clergy.

Then came the final blow—the Expulsion. For reasons best known to himself and his advisers, Carlos III decided to expel the Jesuits from the whole of the Spanish empire. The edict fell in 1767. All missionaries and other Black Robes in New Spain were arrested, dispossessed, hurried to Veracruz, carried to Spain, imprisoned there, or distributed in other lands. Many of the expatriates died of disease or hardship on the way. Some of the missions thus left vacant were secularized, others were put in charge of the Franciscans. Here is where Serra comes into the California story. A work of two centuries was at an end. . . .

The Black Robe story is one of Homeric quality. It is filled with picturesque men, like Santarén, who vied with the Pied Piper of Hamelin; Ruiz, who was arrowproof; Azpilcueto, who bluffed an Indian horde with blunderbuss and machete; Contreras, who led the defense of Cocóspera against an Apache attack; Kino, the hard-riding cowman; Glandorff, the Black Robe hiker with the magic shoes. The tale is full of diverting humor and of exalting edification. The actors were human beings, who either had a sense of humor or were humorous because they lacked it.

These missionaries were the adventurers of the seventeenth and eighteenth centuries, successors to the conquistadores of an earlier day. They traveled vast distances, coped with rugged nature and the fickle savage, performed astounding physical feats, won amazing victories over mountains, rivers, hunger, cold, and thirst.

Missionary life demanded the highest qualities of manhood—character, intelligence, courage, resourcefulness, health, and endurance. Missionaries were called upon to face physical dangers and hardships almost beyond belief. They went among heathen without escorts, into places where soldiers dared not tread. They were liable at any time to hear the blood-curdling war whoop or to see the destroying fire by night. They were ever at the mercy of the whims of sensitive Indians, or of jealous and vengeful medicine men. Even to baptize a child was often perilous, for if it died the death might be charged to the "bad medicine" of the padre. Martyrdom was always a very distinct possibility. Most Black Robes came to America hoping to win this glorious crown, many still coveted it after seeing real Indians, and when martyrdom stared them in the face they met it with transcendent heroism.

Their hardest trial, more to be feared than death, was loneliness, for they lived many leagues apart and saw their own kind only at long intervals. Hence they treasured visits from distant neighbors, and looked forward with the eagerness of a homesick boy to the church dedications and celebrations which brought them for a brief time together; or to the annual journey to a neighbor mission to fulfill their religious obligations. . . .

A catalogue of the manifold services of the missionaries would be long and varied. In their daily routine, like the monks of old, they performed the most menial tasks. They cooked, washed, plowed, planted, harvested, handled stock, made adobes, built houses, and erected churches. They served as nurses and doctors in the huts of natives. During epidemics they were called from pillar to post, lacking time even to eat or sleep. "For in these missions," says Father Neumann, "there is but one craftsman: the missionary himself. He alone must serve both himself and others. He must be cobbler, tailor, mason, carpenter, cook, nurse for the sick—in a word, everything."

The Black Robes converted the natives to Christianity, baptizing in New Spain alone, before the Expulsion, probably not less than two millions. They also brought to the Indians the rudiments of Christian civilization, teaching them decent habits, agriculture, stock raising, the handicrafts, building, and myriad other things. The less civilized natives were the ones most remolded by mission life. . . .

The Black Robes performed many services for the border Spaniards as well as for the neophytes. The mission was the agricultural unit for a large part of frontier Spanish America. There the missionary organized and directed most of the agricultural labor. The mission not only raised produce for its own subsistence, but from the surplus it supplied neighboring soldiers, miners, and cattlemen with agricultural products. The missionaries, by

gentle means, subdued and managed the Indians, went as
diplomats to hostile tribes, and helped to pacify the frontier in time of trouble. The mission itself, with its fortified
plant and its usually loyal native defenders, often served as
a bulwark against hostile neighbors. Regarding frontier
matters, religious or secular, including international relations, the missionaries helped to mold the opinions of
central officials, and were often called to Mexico, or even
to Spain and Rome, to give advice. Instructions issued
from Europe on such matters were both shaped and interpreted by the men on the frontier, for they were the
ones who best knew conditions. . . .

Incidentally to their frontier work they were explorers,
cartographers and ethnologists. Ribas declared them lin-
guists by divine gift, and certain it is that they did much
to reduce to grammar and to preserve the languages of
many tribes, some of which have long since disappeared.

8

Bailey W. Diffie

THE FOUNDATIONS OF
JESUIT POWER

The amazing interplay between spiritual achievements, capacity for organization, and material wealth is bound to puzzle every observer of the Jesuit order, making it difficult for him to arrive at a definitive assessment. An effort of making such an assessment, however, is presented here.

Bailey W. Diffie, who was born in Texas in 1902, took his Ph.D. in history in Spain. He is also an experienced economist. Since 1946 he has been a teacher of Latin-American history at the City College of New York. His textbook Latin American Civilization: the Colonial Period *offers a stimulating and original approach to its subject. As the present excerpt will show, however, it is not free of anachronistic judgments such as criticizing the Jesuits for not having produced a mass-education system.*

From Bailey W. Diffie, *Latin American Civilization: the Colonial Period* (Harrisburg, Pa., 1945), excerpts from pp. 583-587. Reprinted with the permission of Prof. B. W. Diffie and The Stackpole Company, publishers, formerly Stackpole Sons.

The Jesuits, owing to the extent and number of their missions, their schools, and their influence on the intellectual life of the colonies, represent the Church at its most effective usefulness. As missionaries they were among the most daring, as educators among the most assiduous, and as organizers the most efficient. Several factors favored their development. Expressly founded to combat the heresies of the Protestant Revolution, their organization was modeled on that of the Spanish army in the days of its ascendancy; their aim was to convert or reconvert through the medium of education; they had a centralized society whose world-wide activities were directed from one center; and they adopted a collectivistic economy that made the resources of one belong to all.

Not the least of the virtues of the Jesuits was the freedom of their convents[1] from the factionalism and brawls that so often disturbed the other religious communities. Whereas many of the Orders elected their own superiors, the Jesuit leaders were appointed by the General in Rome. This was particularly important in America, where many conflicting currents made the periodical elections a source of constant friction. The internal discipline of the Jesuits was much stricter than in most of the other Orders and they were more nearly free of scandals arising from sexual irregularity. They gained thereby a reputation for morality that was based too largely on chastity and ignored the broader aspects of ethical conduct.

Their educational institutions in the colonies generally enjoyed greater reputation than those of their rivals, and among their members were some of the leading scholars of the age, the most famous teachers, and the most eloquent preachers. Their libraries were reputed the finest.

On the other hand, they never endowed the colonies with an extensive and intensive educational system. Their schools, like those of the other orders, housed a tiny portion of the total number of children, chiefly those who

---

[1] *Convents* is not the appropriate term so far as the Jesuits are concerned. They live in colleges, missions, "residentiæ" or professed houses [ed.]

could pay for their education. Their libraries were composed mainly of works on theology, scholastic philosophy, the writings of Church fathers, treatises on the ethics of the confessional, ecclesiastical legislation, lives of saints, accounts of miracles, and other matters of no practical value to the masses of the people. Most of these works were in Latin, and therefore available to only a small elite. The few works in their libraries on classical antiquity, history, geography, and science were usually outdated, and in the eighteenth century books of the new learning seldom found their way into Jesuit libraries.

Where they exerted a tremendous influence on the colonies was in their strict observance of the forms of religion. They were the most indefatigable preachers, not only in their own missions and monasteries, but in the convents of the nuns, in the churches, and in the jails. They had created numerous religious societies (*cofradías*). They held frequent religious celebrations, and processions organized with great pomp to impress the masses, who found in these activities one of the chief forms of diversion.

Most powerful in influencing the community was their wealth. They had devised ways of inducing legacies and grants for their Order that were characteristic of their efficiency. They honored with the name of "founder" those who endowed a new convent or school, and "benefactor" those who made contributions to the same ends. For each of these they had two grades of spiritual benefits, the funerals, masses, and other honors being more or less pretentious according to the amount of the donation. But they were not dependent on private gifts alone. They received grants from the municipalities and from the governors of the various colonies. With the establishment of a new town they were usually ceded one side of the public square and extensive farm lands. Also, because of their powerful financial position, they were frequently in a position to buy up cheaply rural and urban property that was forced on the market by bankruptcy.

Slaves were among the most valuable possessions of the Jesuits. A close inventory would probably reveal that they owned thousands. That their treatment of the slaves was in keeping with the customs of the times is indicated by the stocks, chains, and other instruments of punishment found on their plantations at the time of their expulsion.

Their efficiency was displayed in the management of great fortunes. Unlike many of the other orders, each Jesuit congregation owned and managed its own properties, although it was required to make extensive donations to the central organization. The produce from their plantations and urban properties, which was actually the product of the work of slaves or mission Indians, was sold in local markets or exported to increase the Order's revenues. To avoid dependence on ordinary commercial channels, they established their own warehouses and stores, and certain of their members accompanied the goods to market. The complaints of rival merchants and the scandals produced by this commercialism caused Viceroy Amat of Peru to issue an order that the Jesuit merchants from Chile and Quito residing in Lima should return to their own provinces because they were engaged in "the sordid exercise of commerce or trade which they carry on openly in the public squares, streets, and markets, to the astonishment of the laity, and in the stores in their own convents, visiting at all hours, in order to make collections, taverns, public houses, and dives of the lowest sort whose business is of the most indecent."

Other types of business they engaged in included rope-making, pottery, textiles, tanneries, and shipbuilding. They may also be accredited with the invention of the *tienda de raya*, or company store, of such dubious fame in modern times. On their plantations they had stores in which their workmen and the local population traded.

And there were other sources of revenue. They collected fees for the various types of religious services rendered to individuals or the state. Missionary work in country districts was paid for by the bishops; frontier missions were supported by the Crown; the children who attended their schools paid fees; and the King paid the tuition of the Indian children in some of their schools. Whenever they suffered destruction of property because of Indian wars or other reasons, they appealed to the authorities and the Crown to recompense them, on the grounds that they were rendering a public service. Not the least among their resources was the privilege of tax exemption, which enabled them to compete with the secular merchants and other plantation owners on extremely favorable grounds.

They also established a form of collectivism, in which the members of the Order, but no others, participated. On entering the Order each member surrendered his personal property and was never allowed to own anything for himself. All of their economic strength was thus centered. This fact also contributed, no doubt, to their reputation for morality. In many of the other orders and among the secular priests there was no prohibition against private property,[2] and it was not unusual to see a priest or monk carrying on private trade, accumulating a fortune, and passing on his property to his relatives, among whom might be numbered his children.

When measured purely as an economic and commercial organization, the Society of Jesus commands admiration. They were the nearest thing in their age to modern chain stores and efficient manufacturers. Their membership was drawn from all nations, and among those who arrived in America were a considerable number who introduced arts and crafts or improved processes, hitherto unknown. Their agricultural methods, and their skill in irrigation, were models for the times. They enjoyed the same advantages as a great modern corporation in centralized administration, command of large capital, and even the ability to avoid taxation by using the ultimate legal technicality devised by the highest-priced lawyers. In sum, the Jesuits had acquired a position and standing in the Spanish colonies (and the world in general) that made them a state within other states, and their power transcended national boundaries. This was the character of the entire church organization, of course, but the efficiency of the Jesuits made them outstanding. Had they not aspired to even greater power they would not have been human, and had they not employed for the purpose the allegedly divine character of their mission they would have been angels.

---

[2] Certainly all members of monastic orders take the vow enforcing personal poverty [ed.].

It was inevitable sooner or later that such a mighty organization should come into head-on conflict with the state. The secular princes (and the Pope himself) believed that Jesuit ambitions included the elimination of all other powers. This may or may not have been true, but it was the motivation on which the monarchs of Europe acted. They were inspired, too, by the eighteenth-century ideas of liberalism, and the desire to tighten the strings of their own authority. The Marquis of Pombal had expelled the Jesuits from Portugal in 1759-60; Louis XV had done the same in France in 1764. Charles III of Spain followed suit in 1767.

In the Spanish colonies the expulsion was greeted with mixed feelings. Some of the other orders scarcely concealed their pleasure; and some, particularly the nuns, were grief-stricken. The Carmelite nuns of Santiago, Chile, for example, placed the image of their patroness, Santa Teresa, on the altar, covered her with a black shawl, and refused to hear either mass, music, or sermon, threatening never to worship Santa Teresa again if the Jesuits were not restored. But the expulsion was carried out without serious opposition and with extraordinary speed and efficiency.

When the excitement and furor of the Jesuit expulsion had died down, and inventory could be taken, it was discovered that their accomplishments were not as solid as supposed. The Indians in their missions soon fell back into a barbarism from which, in truth, they had never been raised. The missions of Paraguay disappeared, as did those of other regions. Some were taken over by other orders, only to reveal that the alleged great number of converted Indians did not exist, or that they knew but little more of Christianity than the unconverted Indians. The Franciscans who took over the missions of Chile reported that the Indians "were as little enlightened, as destitute of instruction and of even the fundamental truths of Christianity, and as settled in the gross ignorance of their errors, superstitions, and barbarous customs, as the other nations of savages who never saw a missionary."

9

François Chevalier

THE FORMATION OF THE JESUIT WEALTH

◇◇◇◇◇◇◇◇◇◇◇◇

How did the Jesuits in Latin America acquire their properties? What was the extent of their holdings? These questions have often been asked and discussed, but seldom on a basis of facts. It would, moreover, be difficult to penetrate these problems if kept isolated from the related aspects of the colonial economy as such which form their natural context. And the agrarian economy of seventeenth- and eighteenth-century Latin America is a subject which has seldom been touched by serious research. One of the few exceptions is the excellent work, solid as well as vivid, on the formation of the Mexican latifundios *by François Chevalier, originally published in French in 1949.*

Born in 1914, the author belongs to a group of dynamic, ingenious economic and social historians formed by Marcel Bloch and Lucien Febvre. After having directed the Institut Français d'Amérique Latine in Mexico City between 1942 and 1962, Chevalier is now teaching Latin-American history at the University of

From François Chevalier, *Land and Society in Colonial Mexico* (Berkeley and Los Angeles, Calif., 1963), excerpts from pp. 229-231, 239-250. Reprinted with the permission of the University of California Press.

*Bordeaux. His treatment of the Jesuits in his magnum
opus is a detailed one, characterized by his calm and
unprejudiced approach and by the richness of his
source material.*

T he first missionaries to arrive in New Spain were almost without exception apostles whose sole, burning
desire was to spread the Gospel. . . . They naturally,
and passionately, protected the Indians against encomenderos or settlers ready to prey upon the helpless. In the
opinion of some conquistadors, they acted like dangerous
revolutionaries, preaching racial equality from their pul-
pits and inciting natives to shake off the semi-illegal yoke
of the encomienda. Such are the reasons for their great
prestige and the scope and speed of their "spiritual conquest," which Robert Ricard has described.

The magnitude of their success was in itself a danger.
The Indians, with the overwhelming gratitude characteristic of the weak and humiliated, offered their saviors land,
legacies, and other gifts. The temptation to acquire
worldly goods was a strong one, not for personal enrich-
ment certainly, but to ensure a monastery or an order the
material security that would spare it from living precari-
ously on alms or government subsidies. The Franciscans
alone generally resisted. . . .

Then a recently founded religious order, differing from
all the others, implanted itself in the country: the Society
of Jesus. After founding schools in the cities (at the close
of the sixteenth century), its members gradually pushed
on with their chain of missions into the huge northwestern
territories. The Society soon complemented its rigid internal discipline with a solid economic organization, which its
rule did not forbid. At the very time when the other orders' zeal was showing signs of abating, the Society's high
principles and the undeniable superiority of its educational
system won for it powerful friends among the nobility
and the rich Spanish or Creole miners and merchants
whose sons were attending its schools. Twenty or thirty
years after the Jesuits' arrival (1572), few wills were being
drawn up that did not provide for them generously; their

novices were being recruited from the wealthiest families, and innumerable gifts and endowed masses were bringing them in large sums of money.

In this relatively poor country, the improvidence and wastefulness of encomenderos, as well as that of miners' and high officials' heirs, amazed contemporaries. "This country's children are so prodigal that they spend every cent they own," the Mexico City administration remarked in 1637. The same document contains a denunciation of the monasteries' wealth. The Church was merely managing its fortune with greater skill. As in medieval Europe, its branches constituted the only closely knit organizations in Mexican society. Its individual representatives were usually the best-educated and most capable members of that society. And, finally, it had tenure in the form of mortmain.

Much of the Church's money went for construction, as shown by the countless monasteries and convents, churches and chapels, whose towers and cupolas betray the smallest Mexican village's presence to a traveler still some distance away. Buildings and altarpieces were all very well, but they were not productive capita assets. If the orders, which collected no tithes, did not wish to remain dependent on private charity or royal subsidies, they would have to assure themselves a regular income by investing to advantage sums coming their way. For those seeking stability and security rather than big profits, there was only one possible investment, land. . . .

The Jesuits were undoubtedly the greatest farmers of all. Many of them were agronomists, and the Society's colleges owned the best-operated, most thriving estates in the viceroyalty. Only the order's professed house vowed to live strictly on alms. . . . The Society was the cleverest of all the orders in finding rich benefactors, such as the famous "Croesus" of New Spain, Alonso de Villaseca; this dry, matter-of-fact businessman, taciturn and of a forbidding appearance, handed over to the Society, before his death in 1580, sums totaling 224,791 pesos (according to his somewhat disgruntled grandson, whose entail had decreased in value). In particular, he founded the Jesuit college in Mexico City with 40,000 pesos in the form of 41 ingots of silver.

He had enough money left to bequeath his daughter a large estate.

Villaseca gave the Jesuits advice that was worth more to them than all his gifts, in the words of a Jesuit who had known him: The best investments for supporting their colleges were "half-completed rural haciendas." The haciendas' unfinished state would keep the sale price low, and the Jesuits' improvements would turn them into valuable assets. Villaseca's own fortune offering proof of his business acumen, the Society followed his recommendations to the letter. Because of the colleges' utility, Viceroy Martín Enriquez closed his eyes to what took place; he even granted the Society many favors in the gruff, offhand manner of its earlier benefactor.

In 1576, the Jesuits' first college, St. Peter and St. Paul in Mexico City, acquired for less than 20,000 pesos a large estate situated a few leagues to the north, on which sheep were being raised. The fathers made it into the Santa Lucía hacienda, the most important one of its kind, it seems, in all the northern Indies. The college went on to buy or constitute other estates and sugar refineries that were even larger than Santa Lucía. . . .

Most of the powerful merchants of Mexico City, Puebla, or the big mining camps became at one time or another the Jesuits' friends and benefactors. Alvaro de Lorenzana, whom a contemporary described as "one of the richest men ever to be seen in this kingdom or anywhere else" (his liquid assets alone were said to total 800,000 pesos), not only served as patron of the Convent of the Incarnation and endowed eight cathedral prebends in Mexico City, but appointed the Jesuits executors of his will and, naturally, did not fail to remember them therein (1651). Martin Ruiz de Zavala, a member of the northern family whose miners and merchants were nearly all outstanding Church benefactors, supplied funds for the founding of the college at San Luis Potosí in 1620.

The landed aristocracy was not so generous, probably because it had less money; its entails were, by definition, indivisible and often in a bad state. It welcomed, moreover, alliances with the rich merchant class. Because of so much intermarriage, it is hard for us to determine to which category certain benefactors belong, for example, a powerful man like Juan de Chavarría.

The secular clergy, too, answered the Jesuits' appeals most generously. Clergymen's fortunes were more modest than merchants', to be sure; but the most insignificant prebendaries usually had good incomes and, owing to their vow of celibacy, fewer heirs. In the early days, vicars, canons, and ordinary clerics—even prelates and wealthy cathedral chapters—bestowed upon the Jesuits a striking number of gifts and legacies. . . . Good relations were unfortunately impaired when the Jesuits asserted that they were exempted from tithing; the dispute culminated in an extremely violent controversy with the venerable Bishop of Puebla, Palafox y Mendoza.

The Society converted its pesos and countless gifts (often of a very humble sort), purchases, and exchanges of land into huge estates and flourishing haciendas. The process is a curious blend of calculation, spontaneity, skill, and force. The Society's temporal activities approach the grandiose; starting from scratch, it soon had the largest flocks of sheep, the finest sugar plantations, and the best-managed estates, not to speak of the indisputable superiority of its colleges and missions.

Firm self-discipline and high moral standards were at the root of the disinterestedness, even the love of poverty, which members of the order revealed in their pursuits. The large sums that they gathered in were spent, not on individuals, but on the betterment of the order; consequently, every peso was made to count. . . .

For a period when the Church was still prohibited from buying, if not from owning, real estate in the Indies, the Jesuits systematically built up their rich estates in an amazingly short time and without difficulty. Relying on their powerful backers and lawyer friends (many of whom had attended their schools), they did not allow obsolescent clauses in title deeds to deter them from attaining ends that they felt justified the means: maintaining their colleges —of whose usefulness there was no question—and aiding their missions in the remotest, most forsaken parts of the viceroyalty. They showed so peculiar a skill in handling men, whether Spaniards or Indians, and so keen a business sense in acquiring, managing, and utilizing to the utmost their worldly possessions that an Italian, Gemelli Carreri, remarked, apropos the northern missions, that the Jesuits were "more ingenious than the other missionaries in looking out for themselves." . . .

[Jesuit] colleges frequently used friends and third parties for delicate negotiations in which they preferred not to figure directly, seeing that they had no legal right to own land. In 1594, a man was granted two sheep estancias. Two years later, he made them over to the Society. In 1607, acting as if he still owned them, he requested the Viceroy's permission to use them for cattle. He was clearly a dummy for the real owner, the College of St. Peter and St. Paul. In spite of opposition from an Indian municipality and two encomenderos, the local alcalde (mayor) approved conversion of one of the estancias. Actually, the fathers did not scruple to raise horses and mules on land officially reserved for sheep, even when permission was denied them.

In many regions, the Society did not attempt to conceal the fact that, acting through proxies, it was obtaining needed land from the Viceroy. . . . The Jesuits had no monopoly on such irregularities. However, their greater zeal and method in bridging the gap between theoretical inability to own any land whatsoever and the actual acquisition of vast holdings gave rise to the greatest variety of legal subterfuges; some of them were curious, even unexpectedly comical. The viceregal administration could hardly continue to feign ignorance. It acknowledged the holdings' existence on several occasions; in 1581 and 1583, for example, it confirmed their exemption from the tithe. The authorities' tolerance was also tacit admission of the great services rendered by Jesuit colleges, which charged no tuition. The Jesuits' rural estates, furthermore, were self-supporting—except for their northern missions—unlike those of other orders whose revenues were not so flourishing. Favors granted the Society by local major and minor officials show that, by the turn of the century, it enjoyed considerable standing throughout New Spain.

All the Society's blocks and parcels of land—large and small, purchased or donated, tilled or fallow—were

grouped according to region and made into large, prosperous estates at a tempo depending on the region. Like some
medieval monasteries, colleges spent generous sums on
equipping their estates with the best livestock and farm
implements available, stout outbuildings (still in use today), and especially, plentiful crews of Indian day laborers, and even Negro slaves on their sugar plantations. They
plowed and seeded the best land, leaving arid or less fertile
expanses for sheep pasture. . . .

Some colleges' estates formed compact masses; others
were located in more than one region. Around 1670, for
example, the seminary at Tepotzotlán, north-northwest of
Mexico City, owned large haciendas in its home territory; but it also had holdings around Colima, Sombrerete,
and other New Galicia localities. Dispersal was sometimes
due to chance donations. At other times it was deliberate, as in Colima, where certain colleges had acquired
winter pastures for the immense flocks in which they
specialized. The Tepotzotlán seminary obtained a royal
order allowing its tens of thousands of migrating sheep to
graze on the fallow and stubbled fields in New Spain
"without anyone's gainsaying."

Complementary holdings appear to have been often
grouped in accordance with a plan which would supply
a given religious community with some of all the country's
diversified products. That is probably the explanation of
colleges' many exchanges, sales, and resales until they had
exactly the land that suited their purposes.

Although estates were to keep on growing, they were
already large by the middle of the seventeenth century.
The College of St. Peter and St. Paul in Mexico City possessed the richest. Its Santa Lucía y Nuestra Señora de
Loreto hacienda was one of the biggest sheep-raising centers in the Indies; it was surrounded by a string of smaller
farms and estancias, also the college's property. The college possessed besides three sugar refineries, among the
most important in the country. . . .

Unlike many private landowners, the Society was interested not in cornering all the land in a given region solely
to eliminate competition but in operating its enterprises
at maximum efficiency. If it would support colleges and

missions that were growing in importance daily, it had to keep constantly increasing its revenues, capital investment, and assets. The Jesuits tried to organize land exploitation on a rational basis. . . . Around the end of the sixteenth century, the Society's General in Rome, Father Claudio Acquaviva, did not think it beneath him to have special instructions drawn up for New Spain. He dealt not only with such questions as the proper way to celebrate Mass or what relations should be with vicars residing on rural haciendas, but also the appropriate conduct to observe with servants and farm hands, agrarian economy, and even the best methods of planting and cultivating sugar cane. He especially advised provincials and rectors to follow local farming practice: "Experience is the mother of science," and no individual must take it upon himself to invent clever new agricultural methods. . . .

The most complete document of the sort which we possess, however, is the "Instructions to be observed by Brothers in charge of Administering Rural Haciendas." The *Instrucción,* issued in the second quarter of the eighteenth century, summarized and completed previous ordinances; it thus codified the experience that the Jesuits had accumulated in 150 years of farming in New Spain. The text is a long one—twenty chapters—regulating in minute detail every phase of hacienda administration: spiritual, moral, social, economic, and technical. . . . Special attention was devoted to bookkeeping and record filing. Each administrator was charged with having his clerk keep as many as eight sets of books for the estate under his responsibility: a rough and a clean copy of cash receipts and disbursements, and ledgers for "sowing and harvesting," hiring workers, keeping account of their wages, general inventories, land and water deeds, and debits and credits. The order's rigid discipline made application of every rule a certainty. To judge by what is left of its archives, its workers seem to have been better treated, its accounts better kept, its livestock and equipment of better quality, and its sugar refineries' production above average; these last sold 20,000 to 24,000 loaves (200 to 250 tons) without speeding up the output per worker. . . .

So much concern with haciendas and Mammon made

individual brothers and even college communities run the risk of forsaking the ways of the Lord. Some administrators had to be expelled from the order for violating their vows, in particular the vow of chastity. . . .

The order's provincial purchasing department traded in cattle on a large scale. More shocking to some, the College of St. Peter and St. Paul alone bought or sold more than 500 Negro slaves (carried on their books as "items") in the course of the seventeenth century. . . .

Transactions such as these were the logical, inevitable outcome of exploiting haciendas, droves, weaving mills, and sugar plantations. The Bishop of Puebla, Don Juan de Palafox y Mendoza, in 1647 scathingly denounced the Jesuits' accumulated wealth in a letter to the Pope. He considered it indecent that two colleges should own 300,-000 sheep, as well as cattle, and that the Society itself should own six large sugar plantations in New Spain worth 500,-000 to 1,000,000 pesos apiece and bringing in incomes of as much as 100,000 pesos, prosperous haciendas four to six leagues across, besides factories, shops, and slaughterhouses, and that it should carry on trade with China by way of the Philippines. The Bishop felt that each day its power bred more power and its riches more riches.

The author's tone was vituperative. In his indignation, he failed to add that the Jesuits' personal lives were plain and frugal and that their money went primarily for offering a superior kind of education free of charge. The figures that the Bishop quoted were not exaggerated, however; one sugar refinery was worth 700,000 pesos in the seventeenth century. Some of the Society's arguments in rebuttal were not very convincing; for example, it claimed that colleges had small endowments or even "live in straitened circumstances." The debts that it was constantly pleading were essentially fees due on property recently acquired or loans designed to improve its haciendas and cover the costs of its numerous sturdily constructed buildings. It methodically paid the fees and repaid the loans; but at the same time it incurred new ones by acquiring more land and making more improvements. Over a thirty-four-year period, St. Peter and St. Paul's spent 380,000 pesos to amortize 176 loans, fee payments, and mortgages; in the same period, the college contracted new debts "for the out-fitting of its haciendas and plantations." Actually, the Society's holdings never stopped growing and were larger than ever in the eighteenth century.

The wealth of most of the colleges cannot be doubted, although their estates' earning power was hampered by inadequate markets. The Jesuits undeniably carried on various economic and commercial activities. Just as undeniably, their striving for worldly possessions was a way of strengthening the order's independence, social influence, and political power.

The whole Society, still a youth among orders, had kept the vitality and powerful self-discipline drilled into it by its founders, as witness the wonderful missions in New Viscaya and Lower California. . . . To a greater extent than the other orders, the Jesuits, in their task of converting the natives, were concerned with improving living conditions and developing the missions' economic activities. Father Kino taught various native tribes in the northwest how to raise cattle; they owned immense herds, and he not a single cow. Avoiding the medieval Templars' errors, the Jesuits did maintain, in the seventeenth century, a perfect balance between their worldly pursuits and their order's spiritual aims. Furthermore, their understanding of economics, their business sense, and their efficient exploitation of landed property struck a relatively new and discordant note in the Indies, where so many hidalgos and cattle barons were disdainful of economics.

10

Charles Ralph Boxer

MISSIONARIES, COLONISTS, AND INDIANS IN AMAZONIA

The long struggle between colonists and Jesuits in Maranhão and Pará for control over the Indian manpower is probably the most important antecedent for the expulsion of the Jesuits from the Portuguese realm, in its turn the first step toward the world-wide abolition of the Society of Jesus in 1773. As a change from all the biased interpretations of this conflict, the following text will offer a balanced view based on primary sources.

C. R. Boxer, born in Great Britain in 1904, is a remarkable scholar of a rather unusual kind. Until 1947 he pursued a military career, fighting against the Japanese during the second world war. At the same time he became a specialist on the history of the Far East with particular attention to the role of the Portuguese. When he retired as a major he became Camões Professor of Portuguese at the University of London. His numerous works include an excellent book, The Christian Century in Japan, 1549-1640 *(1951), in which*

From C. R. Boxer, *The Golden Age of Brazil, 1695-1750: Growing Pains of a Colonial Society* (Berkeley and Los Angeles, Calif., 1962), excerpts from pp. 277-295. Reprinted with the permission of the University of California Press.

the Jesuits play the principal role. As a result of his interest in Portuguese imperialism, Professor Boxer has dealt with Brazil as well as with the Far East. He has devoted some books to the seventeenth-century history of Brazil; however, the one which contains the text reproduced here deals with the first half of the eighteenth century. Few scholars are able to base their observations of the Jesuits and their role within Portuguese colonial society on such a wide range of research and observation.

The Jesuits alone among the religious orders in Brazil had a consistent tradition of upholding the freedom of the Amerindians against all the efforts of the colonists to enslave and exploit them. . . . The colonists, supported intermittently by the friars, reacted vigorously in kind, alleging that the Jesuits merely wished to deprive them of their Amerindian laborers in order to exploit them for their own purposes. The Crown, by and large, sympathized with the Jesuits' stand, but could not afford to ignore entirely the protests of the colonists and the friars. The laws which were framed at Lisbon to protect the Amerindians were thus inevitably of a compromise character which satisfied none of the parties to the dispute. . . .

The perennial disagreements between the Jesuits and the colonists over the treatment of the Amerindians in Amazonia twice resulted in the forcible expulsion of those missionaries in a manner which gave some justification to Padre António Vieira's characterization of Maranhão-Pará as Portugal's La Rochelle.[1] On the first occasion (1661-62) the Jesuits were expelled from the whole state, but on the second (1684) from the Maranhão only, Belem having declined to follow the lead of São Luís, owing to the increasing rivalry between the two cities. Deprived of the support of Pará, the Maranhão was easily subdued on the arrival of a new governor, who executed two of the ringleaders in

---

[1] La Rochelle is a French seaport town, historically famous as a Protestant stronghold until it was forced to surrender in 1628 [ed.].

November 1685. Abortive as it proved, the revolt of 1684 helped to convince the Jesuits that they must compromise with the colonists' need for forced labor to a greater extent than they had done hitherto. The result was embodied in the *Regimento das Missões do Estado do Maranhão e Grão-Pará*, promulgated by the Crown in 1686. With certain alterations and modifications introduced between 1688 and 1718, this *Regimento* formed the basic charter for missionary work and for the supply of Amerindian labor in the state of Maranhão-Pará until the secularization of the missions by the Crown in 1750-1755.

One of the principal provisions of the law of 1686 was that in the future Amerindian labor would be increasingly supplanted by a regular supply of Negro slaves from Guinea, by means of a slave-trading company which was formed for this specific purpose. In the upshot, this company was stillborn, and the need for Amerindian labor remained paramount. As envisaged by the final decree of 1718, this labor was to be secured in two ways: peaceful and forceful. The peaceful expeditions were to be organized by the missionaries, who would seek out the unsubdued tribes in the jungle and try to convince them that they would be better off living as "rational men" in mission villages (*aldeias*) under the superintendency of the Jesuits, or of the other religious orders, and in the vicinity of the white settlements. Those who freely consented to this course were to be brought down from the interior, but they were not to be enslaved on any account, and were to receive regular and adequate wages, in addition to their keep and clothing for any work they performed for the colonists. Once settled in the *aldeias*, they were to be taught the rudiments of Christianity and civilized ways for two years before being made available for employment by white men.

The second, or forceful, method was to be employed against those savage tribes who went completely naked, recognized no king nor form of government, and who persistently indulged in unnatural vices such as incest and cannibalism. These barbarians, so the Crown was assured by learned theologians, could be forcibly settled in mission villages on two conditions. Firstly, that only the necessary minimum of force should be used, and then only after

peaceful persuasion had failed and the savages had re-
sorted to arms to defend their bestial way of life. Secondly, those who were forcibly settled in the *aldeias*, but
who subsequently fled back to the jungle to resume their
uncivilized life, could be pursued and recaptured, but they
were not on any account to be killed. Expeditions made
under such conditions were entitled justifiable and defen-
sive wars; but they were not to be undertaken without the
prior approval of the representatives of the religious orders
as well as of the senior Crown authorities. Unauthorized
raiding by the colonists was categorically forbidden.

The mission villages as they developed in the early eighteenth century . . . were grouped into four main categories. First, those that were organized solely for the service
and benefit of the religious order to which they were assigned. Second, those of the Crown, whose inmates provided labor for the public works such as fortifications,
shipbuilding, salt pans, and fisheries. Third, those termed
of the *Repartição*, which provided labor for the colonists
who needed hands for their houses, plantations, sugar mills,
and canoes. Fourth and last were the purely mission villages
in the far interior, remote from any contact with white
laymen, where the missionaries' only object was to convert and civilize the Amerindians. All these types of *aldeias* were, in principle, economically self-supporting,
and all were directly supervised by a couple of missionaries from the order to which they belonged. No laymen
could visit a mission village without permission from the
superior authority, and all requests from the colonists for a
supply of free Amerindian labor had to be referred to the
missionaries of the locality concerned.

Regulations for the conduct and administration of the
Jesuits' *aldeias* were drawn up by Padre António Vieira,
S.J., about the year 1660, and they lasted substantially unchanged until the secularization of the mission villages
nearly a century later. . . . The surplus produce of the
mission villages was marketed by lay agents at Belem
and São Luís (on a commission basis, presumably). The
proceeds were remitted to the village concerned, for the
upkeep of the church and the hospital and the like, after
paying for such goods as the villagers might require from

those two cities. . . . Full registers were kept in each village of all births, baptisms, marriages, and deaths; special
care being exercised in marriage between a free Amerindian and a slave woman, "these marriages, under the
pretense of matrimony, being one of the means of enslavement which is used in this State." . . . The employment of
the mission Indians by the Crown officials and the colonists
was hedged about with numerous safeguards. . . . The
missionaries were exhorted "to insist on the proper payment for the sweat of these poor wretches, since the conversion of those who are still heathen depends on the
good treatment accorded to those who are already Chris-
tians." Rigid restrictions were laid on the employment
of women from the *aldeias*, whose services could only be
hired on one of the following four conditions: (1) as
wet nurses; (2) as elderly maidservants allotted to senior
government and ecclesiastical officials; (3) as maids to poor
and respectable white women who had no other resource;
(4) in limited numbers and with their respective husbands
at the time of the manioc harvest.

Despite the protective nature of the Crown regulations
concerning the domestication of savage tribes, and despite
the paternal authority enjoyed by the Jesuits and the other
orders administering the labor force of the *aldeias*, abuses
in securing and employing Amerindian labor continued
throughout the first half of the eighteenth century. . . .
The principal culprits were, as often as not, the governors
of Maranhão-Pará, among whom Christovão da Costa
Freire (1707-1718) set a particularly bad example. He not
only misused his authority by sending slaving expeditions
into the interior on his own behalf, "but likewise gives free
license to all others who wish to do so, contrary to the stipu-
lations of Your Majesty's laws." These slave raiders did
not, of course, ostensibly act as such. On the contrary, they
asserted that they were merely engaged in peacefully persuading the savages to return with them to the vicinity of
the white settlements. They did not scruple on at least one
occasion to disguise one of their number as an influential
missionary! Where such deceitful measures failed, the
slavers indulged in aggressive forays against unsubdued
(but often inoffensive) tribes, pleading that they were only

acting in self-defense to preserve their own lives from the attacks of ferocious cannibals.

Under the regulations of 1688-1691, the official expeditions (*entradas, resgates*) into the interior were supposed to be accompanied by Jesuit missionaries who would ensure that only those savages were captured who had been taken in "a just war," or as "Indians of the cord." [2] The Jesuits were loath to undertake this invidious task, and normally excused themselves on the plea that they could not spare their men from their work in the *aldeias*. Some of the friars proved more complacent, but most expeditions were undertaken without any adequate missionary supervision. The captives secured, whether by fighting or barter, were treated as slaves, although a formal decision whether they really were so was postponed until the expedition returned to Belem, usually with only about half of those who had been captured. . . .

Apart from the abuses connected with the *entradas* and *resgates*, whether these latter were official or clandestine, the Jesuits had numerous complaints to make about the way the Amerindians from the mission villages were treated when they were hired out for the service of the Crown officials or of the colonists (*moradores*). Once the natives had been persuaded to leave the jungle and settle in the *aldeias*, both governors and colonists were likely to break the promises concerning the conditions of labor which the missionaries had made on their behalf. Amerindians who had consented to come on condition that they were not conscripted as rowers for official canoes, or for carrying heavy building stone, found that they were soon employed on such hard labor. . . .

The complaints were not, of course, all on one side. The missionaries—and particularly the Jesuits—were accused by some officials and by many colonists of interfering with the Amerindians who were not included in the temporal

---

2 "Indians of the cord" were Indians held as prisoners by other Indians and found tied with cord. Because the law provided that such Indians might be enslaved, the settlers, as Bailey Diffie says, "never seemed to find any other type of Indians when they went on slaving expeditions. Apparently every Indian in the Amazon valley was tied to a stake" [ed.].

jurisdiction which the Crown had granted the religious orders over the mission villages. They were also accused of employing more natives than they were entitled to do in their sugar mills and plantations, in their tobacco fields, in their village industries and in the gathering of the "spices of the forest," while keeping the settlers unduly short of the Amerindian labor they so vitally needed. They were also alleged to shelter military deserters in their upcountry missions, and to engage in trade and commerce to an extent which put the local merchants out of business. . . . Finally, the missionaries were accused of deliberately neglecting to teach their native converts Portuguese, preferring the use of Tupí as a better means of keeping them under their own control and perpetuating the language barrier between them and the settlers. All these complaints were lodged at one time or another against each of the religious orders; but it was always the Jesuits who were the main target for hostile criticism. Not for nothing did Padre António Vieira, S.J., compare Maranhão-Pará with Huguenot La Rochelle; but it was not until the second and third decades of the eighteenth century that this bitter criticism of the Jesuits in Amazonia found powerful supporters in government circles at Lisbon.

The extent of the Jesuits' power and influence in late-seventeenth-century Portugal is an easily verifiable historical fact. Closely connected with the restoration of Portuguese independence, and extremely influential at the court of the first two monarchs of the House of Braganza, their position seemed secure in the early years of the reign of Dom João V. He had been educated by the Jesuits, and he had Jesuit confessors in his youth and for the first seven years of his long reign. From the year 1713 onward, however, he made a point of selecting his own confessors from one of the other religious orders. . . . He seems to have subsidized the Oratorians' educational activities as a deliberate counterweight to the hitherto overwhelming preponderance of the Jesuits in this sphere. Finally, he resolutely opposed the efforts of the Jesuits of the Maranhão-Pará mission to secure their *aldeias* from episcopal visitation and inspection. . . .

The Jesuits' most dangerous enemy was a settler from the Maranhão named Paulo da Silva Nunes. He was patronized by Bernardo Pereira de Berredo, author of the classic *Anais Históricos do Maranhão* (Lisbon, 1749), who governed the state from 1718 to 1722, and who was likewise an ill-wisher to the Society of Jesus. Berredo's successor, João da Maia da Gama, who governed Maranhão-Pará with conspicuous ability and honesty from 1722 to 1728, was an ardent admirer of the Jesuits in general and of Padre Jacinto de Carvalho in particular, and he soon fell foul of da Silva Nunes. After a short spell in jail, the latter made his way to Lisbon, where he became the official representative of the colonists of Maranhão-Pará, and deluged the Overseas Councilors and other influential persons with vicious memorials denouncing the behavior of the Jesuits in Amazonia, until his death in 1746. . . . Paulo da Silva Nunes had the lowest possible opinion of the Amerindians, whom he denounced as "squalid savages, ferocious and most base, resembling the wild beasts in everything save in human shape." He accused the Jesuits of behaving despotically and of usurping the royal authority. They incited colored servants to leave the houses of the whites by whom they had been brought up. They supplied their Amerindian converts with firearms, resulting in the death of several Portuguese. In some *aldeias*, the resident missionary built a prison, into which white men were often thrown in chains. The Jesuits obstructed the efforts of the settlers to secure labor from the *aldeias*, as the colonists were legally entitled to do. Their so-called mission villages looked more like busy customs houses than houses of prayer. Last but not least, they had treasonable dealings with the Spaniards along the upper Amazon, with the Dutch along the upper Río Negro, and with the French along the coast of Guiana.

For some years Silva Nunes' anti-Jesuit propaganda had no great success at Court. His vilification of the Amerindians ran counter to the Crown's conviction (which originated with the Jesuits) that "the security of the backlands and of the very settlements of the Maranhão and of all America depends on the friendship of the Indians." The support which the colonists' champion received from Pe-

reira de Berredo and from Sousa Freire[3] was more than
offset by the testimony of Maia da Gama, who had no
difficulty in exposing the unreliability of his successor's
evidence. . . . A senior official, sent out to investigate the
situation on the spot in 1734-1735, reported favorably on
the religious orders in general and on the Jesuits in particular. He did, however, suggest that the Crown should give
the mission villages direct financial support, and so obviate
the need for the missionaries to gather and export "the
spices of the forest," in order to get the wherewithal for the
upkeep of the *aldeias*. The Crown rejected this recommendation, preferring the existing practice of self-supporting
missions. . . . Nevertheless, the seed so pertinaciously sown
by the Jesuits' opponents on both sides of the Atlantic did
not all fall on stony ground. Some of it came to fruition
soon after the death of Dom João V, when the future Marquis of Pombal and his brother, Francisco Xavier de Mendonça Furtado, reaped where Silva Nunes and Pereira de
Berredo had sown.

That the allegations of the Jesuits' enemies were either
wholly false or else grossly exaggerated there can be no
reasonable doubt. Apart from the evidence of Maia da
Gama and other trustworthy Portuguese, we have the testimony of the French scientist La Condamine, who voyaged
down the Amazon from Jaén to Belem do Pará in 1743. He
contrasted the prosperity of the Portuguese mission villages that he visited on his voyage with the poverty of those
on Spanish territory. On the other hand, it is equally clear
from the same sources, and from eyewitnesses such as the
German Jesuit Samuel Fritz, that the colonists of Maranhão-Pará continued to make clandestine slave raids into the
interior, apart from the so-called ransoming expeditions
(*resgates*) which were authorized, and indeed encouraged,
by the Crown. . . .

Despite the difficulties and setbacks with which the missionaries inevitably had to contend, the first half of the
eighteenth century can fairly be termed the golden age of
the missions in Amazonia. . . . Such few statistics as we

---

[3] Alexandre de Sousa Freire was governor of Maranhão-Pará,
1728-1730 [ed.].

possess reflect the relative prosperity of the missions. In 1696, there were about 11,000 Amerindian converts in the Jesuit *aldeias* alone, a number which had risen to 21,031 by 1730, despite the periodic ravages of smallpox, a disease to which the natives were particularly vulnerable. These Amerindians were divided among some twenty-eight *aldeias*. . . .

During the first half of the eighteenth century, Portuguese enterprise, whether in the form of peaceful penetration by the missionaries or of slave-raiding and slave-trading expeditions by laymen, steadily pushed back the disputed frontier with Spanish territory in the Amazon region. . . . The boundary line between the Spanish and Portuguese possessions in South America still theoretically coincided with that laid down by the Treaty of Tordesillas in 1494. This line was a meridian drawn 370 leagues to the west of the most westerly of the Cape Verde Islands; but for more than two and a half centuries there was no agreement between the two Iberian powers as to where this line ran between the Amazon and the Río de la Plata. By 1746 the rulers at Lisbon and Madrid had belatedly come to realize the need for negotiating a boundary settlement which would take account of what had happened in South America and in the Far East during the last two hundred and fifty years. A private exchange of letters between the two royal families having shown that the prospect of concluding such an agreement was now favorable, the diplomatic negotiations were set afoot which resulted in the conclusion of the Treaty of Madrid four years later. . . .

The Portuguese objectives in negotiating the Treaty of 1750 may be resumed as follows: (1) To strike a balance between the boundary claims of Spain and Portugal by allotting the greater part of the Amazon basin to the latter country and that of the Río de la Plata to the former. (2) To secure the undisputed sovereignty of the gold and diamond districts for the Portuguese Crown. (3) To secure Brazil's frontier by the retention of the Rio Grande do Sul and the acquisition of the Spanish Jesuit mission area ("Seven Peoples") on the left bank of the river Uruguay. (4) To secure the western frontier of Brazil and river communication with Maranhão-Pará by ensuring that navigation on the rivers Tocantins, Tapajos, and Madeira remained in Portuguese hands.

On the Spanish side, the compelling motives seem to have been: (1) To stop the westward advance of the Portuguese, who had already encroached on much of what was theoretically Spanish territory even though it consisted mostly of virgin jungle. (2) To secure the colony of Sacramento, which functioned as a back door for the illegal Anglo-Portuguese trade with the Viceroyalty of Peru and which rendered Buenos Aires dangerously exposed to foreign invasion. (3) To undermine the Anglo-Portuguese alliance, and thus eventually to facilitate a union of the two Iberian powers in South America against English aggression. . . .

Generally speaking, the treaty was framed on the basis of *uti possidetis,* save that the colony of Sacramento was to be handed over to the Spaniards in return for the territory occupied by the "Seven Peoples" of the Jesuit mission stations.[4]

The consequences which flowed from the signing of this treaty lie outside the scope of this book, but the reader may be reminded of three basic facts. Firstly, the implementation of the treaty was surreptitiously opposed by influential people in both Portugal and Spain, and by the Amerindians of the "Seven Peoples" with arms in their hands. Secondly, Pombal's hatred of the Jesuits and his suppression of their Society in Portugal stemmed from his conviction that their machinations were responsible for the stipulated territorial adjustments not being made in Uruguay and Amazonia. Incidentally, Pombal was one of the critics of the treaty, and, while blaming the Jesuits for its failure, he was glad of the excuse to keep the colony of Sacramento and return the ruined missions of Uruguay to the Spaniards by the Treaty of Pardo (1761) which formally annulled that of Madrid. The final settlement which was reached at San Ildefonso in 1777 was basically not very different from that envisaged at Madrid twenty-seven years earlier.

---

[4] *Uti possidetis* (Latin: as you now possess) in international law means that a treaty is based on the actual control of disputed territories. The author's translation of *Os sete povos* seems misleading. "The seven villages (or towns)" would have been more appropriate [ed.].

III

The Expulsion of the
Jesuits from Brazil

11

Luis Gonzaga Jaeger

MANY WERE THE PRETEXTS

The expulsion of the Jesuits from the Portuguese Empire has sometimes been explained mainly with reference to the assassination attempt on King Joseph I and other circumstances in Portugal itself, and at times has been attributed to the age-long conflict between Jesuits and colonists in Brazil. The following text, which makes no claim of being an original interpretation, provides a useful summary of the different factors, both European and South American, which might have dictated Pombal's anti-Jesuit course. The author is a Brazilian Jesuit scholar, Father Luis Gonzaga Jaeger (1889-1963), author of several studies of the history of the Jesuits in Rio Grande do Sul and one of the founders and collaborators of the Instituto Anchietano de Pesquisas of Porto Alegre. What should have become his principal work, a history of the Jesuits in Southern Brazil since the restoration of the Society, was left unfinished at his death. Among the Jesuit historians of Rio Grande do Sul a predecessor

Translated from Luis Gonzaga Jaeger, *A expulsão da Companhia de Jesus do Brasil em 1760. Exame crítico-histórico no seu bicentenário* (Porto Alegre, 1960) which constitutes No. 12 of the historical series of *Pesquisas*, the pamphlets published by the Instituto Anchietano de Pesquisas. By permission of the Director of the Institute, Father Aloysio Sehnem, S.J.

*of Father Gonzaga Jaeger, Carlos Teschauer, the au-
thor of an extensive História do Rio Grande do Sul,
is probably better known.*

At the time of our stay in Portugal (1910-1911) it was
hearsay among the Portuguese Jesuits that Carvalho
had shown in the beginning such a liking for the Fathers of
the Society he even ordered a black cassock, such as that
worn by the Jesuits, for one of his young sons to wear in
public. Surely these must have been the days of King
John V, who did not sympathize with Carvalho during the
period when the latter still begged for the influence of the
sons of Saint Ignatius at Court. Once Carvalho reached
power, however, he "turned coat," as will be shown. His
dislike for the Society grew so intensively that at times it
gave him the aspect of a demoniac fanatic, not stopping
even after he had expelled the Jesuits from the Portuguese
domains. He continued to instigate other Catholic powers
to employ all licit and illicit methods in order to make
those detestable religious disappear from the face of the
earth. The Marquis of Pombal harbored inextinguishable
hatred towards the Society of Jesus. . . . To a despotic
temperament such as that of Sebastião José de Carvalho,
the failure of the transfer of "seven missions" [1] was cause
for real furor. He decided to employ all efforts toward an-
nihilating the powerful enemies, even to the extreme of destroying their very existence.

Let us analyze some of these causes or pretexts, recalling
the old refrain: *"Amicus Plato, sed magis amica veritas"*
(Plato is a friend, but a greater friend is truth).

1. The Treaty of Madrid of 1750. Upon entering office
on August 3, 1750, Carvalho found there was a treaty to be
carried out. It was the so-called Treaty of Madrid of January 13, 1750, accomplished by the great Brazilian, Alexandre de Gusmão, and countersigned by John V. It had been
inspired by the sincere intention of ending once and for all
the discussions and doubts around the Portuguese–Spanish

---

[1] The territory of the seven Guaraní missions which Spain
ceded to Portugal (south of the Uruguay River) in accordance
with the Treaty of 1750 [ed.].

border in South America. The territory of the missions in
Rio Grande do Sul that was to be given to Portugal in
exchange for Colonia do Sacramento on the eastern shore
of the River Plate unfortunately fell exactly into a zone
that was tenaciously contested by both the Spanish and the
Portuguese crown. "There were clauses in this treaty that
were difficult to execute. In one of these clauses there were
conditions not only hard but inhuman," Marcos Carneiro
de Mendonça states with good reason. In fact, the sixteenth
article reads as follows: "From the populations or villages
that His Catholic Majesty cedes on the eastern margin of
the Uruguay River, the missionaries will leave with all their
movable property, taking with them the Indians to settle
them in other Spanish territories. The said Indians may also
take all their movable goods, and the arms, powder, and
ammunition which they possess. In this way the villages,
with all their houses, church, edifices, and the property
thereof, and ownership of the terrain will be given to the
Crown of Portugal. . . ."

In Article 15, dealing with the Colonia do Sacramento,
it was said that the "residents might freely stay on, or go
back to other lands of the Portuguese, with their properties and belongings, selling the real estates." The end of
Article 16 stated: "The properties ceded by His Faithful
Majesty [King of Portugal] and His Catholic Majesty
[King of Spain] on the margins of the rivers Pequeri,
Guaporé, and Amazon will be handed over in the same
manner as the Colonia do Sacramento, as written in Article
14. The Indians of all parts shall have the same liberty to
leave or stay on in the same way, with the same prerogatives as the residents of that fortress, except that those who
leave shall lose the property of the real estates, if they have
any."

Here is a manifest, intended, and calculated double measure: The Indians will leave by will or force; whereas the
others that were affected by the treaty may choose, or even
sell, their properties, thus being reimbursed. For the Guaraní Indians there was no such consideration.

In this treaty two questions immediately arise: In the
first place, the cession or exchange of colonial territories on
the part of two monarchies; and second, the compulsory

expropriation of the collective and individual properties of the Indians together with the change of residence. As for the first point, at the time of absolutism the dominant juridical ideas attributed to the sovereigns the right of renouncing or exchanging territories at their will. So far as the second point is concerned, the following question was raised: Does the King also have the right of depriving his subjects of so many private properties, justly acquired during long decades of work, and forcing them to emigrate to distant regions without any adequate indemnization? They were offered the meager sum of thirty thousand "pesos," that is, one "peso" per inhabitant.

The Father General of the Society of Jesus, foreseeing the terrible storm that was brewing in Europe, and which would soon break over his Company, had given a terminating order to the Jesuits of the Province of Paraguay to carry out the transfer as soon as possible. Some—not all—judging that this law did not bind one's conscience since it was manifest sin, disagreed. But there is no proof that any Jesuit instigated the Indians to oppose the transmigration.

How did the Indians of the seven missions receive such a hard order to leave their lands, inherited from their ancestors and cultivated with such care, along with their immense ranches, their rich farms, their yerba and cotton plantations which together made up their principal source of maintenance, their grandiose temples which had no equal in all America, their small houses so much to their liking and so comfortable, their workshops, their cemeteries with their dear dead? They should abandon all of this? And why? To where would they be expelled? To the desert, to regions already occupied by others? What crime had they committed to deserve such punishment? In one of the answers of the seven principal Indian chiefs given to Andonaegui, Governor of Buenos Aires, the Indians recall that the beasts oppose resistance when one attempts to dislodge them from their caves; how then shall we not do as much if they try to deprive us of everything which is ours?

Let us put ourselves, for a few moments, in the place of the Mission Indian. He had a profoundly telluric sense, if not of country, at least an insurmountable attachment to the homeland, the place that had seen his birth. There are irrefutable proofs of this fact.

Should we expect from the Guaraní of the seven missions an indifference, a stoic insensibility in the face of this transfer which was so contrary to their most sacred interests? What had they to do with the rivalries of two Crowns on the other side of the ocean which now caused them to be expelled from their homes?

Without the cooperation of the Jesuit priests, who until then had helped them in everything, the Indians, under the leadership of the brave Sepe Tiarajú, reacted as real savages, without calm or reflection, and without measuring the consequences. On their part, the Superiors of the Society did everything in their power to avoid the war which, they foresaw, would be terrible for their pupils. They wrote to the King of Spain, but Minister Carvajal carefully confiscated all the Jesuits' correspondence, keeping the monarch in total ignorance of the truth about the missions.

It is certain that the Treaty of 1750 displeased the Portuguese and the Spanish, both feeling that they had been set back. Although the Indians of the seven missions were in part crushed by the Portuguese–Spanish arms, the desired transfer never took place. This provoked an undisguisable indignation, especially in the court of King Joseph I, where Carvalho threw the entire blame of the failure upon the Jesuits. The Spanish historian Francisco Mateos, who thoroughly studied the entire documentation relating to these episodes, reduces the failure to three fundamental errors, all of them foreign to the sons of the Society of Jesus: (1) absolute ignorance of the American reality; (2) total lack of the required tact to carry out the transfer; and (3) incredible rush and haste in its execution. Had there been more tact, more calm, and the indispensable amount of time, the Jesuits would have carried out the transfer to a satisfactory conclusion. But, as the really guilty parties did not want to acknowledge their error, the Portuguese and Spanish men of government hastily excused themselves, throwing all the responsibility upon the Jesuits whom they wanted to destroy. On the other hand, the idea of leaving the Indians of the seven missions where they were, just changing sovereigns, was soon rejected by the Spaniards, who did not want to have in their neighborhood such a powerful and therefore dangerous population. . . .

2. *The Commercial Company of Great-Pará.* Another reason the Portuguese Minister was irked with the Jesuits was because of the negative attitude of many Jesuits towards the recently founded Commercial Company of Great-Pará, which gave Carvalho exclusive rights of navigation, Negro traffic, and sale of colonial products, the prices of which he himself fixed. The complaints were general, especially from those who were harmed, including the Jesuits of the north of Brazil because the monopoly cut their means of adequately supporting their missions. Sebastião José de Carvalho answered with the violence characteristic of his manner: he exiled from the Court some Jesuit Fathers. . . .

3. *The Earthquake of Lisbon, November 1, 1755.* On this date at nine-thirty in the morning, a terrifying earthquake reduced a great part of the city of Lisbon to a hill of ruins, causing the death of eight to ten thousand citizens, innumerable wounded among the inhabitants, and the ruin of properties of incalculable value. In this tragic moment it is undeniable that the omnipotent Minister revealed himself worthy of his office, and, we could almost say, this was the one time when he showed capacity for realization and decision, dynamism, and far-reaching vision, a time when he did not spare himself from work day and night for many long months. Little by little the destroyed city, cleaned of the rubbish, reappeared from the ruins, new, better than before. Unfortunately, Carvalho's ill will towards the Society of Jesus discovered even here a reason to release itself.

The saintly and beloved missionary of Brazil, Father Gabriel de Malagrida, with the necessary permission, published a spiritual paper entitled "Judgment of the Real Cause of the Earthquake which the Court of Lisbon Suffered on November 1, 1755," printed the following year. The paper accused the moral guilts of the people of Lisbon and indirectly the state, making responsible for the disaster not the "contingent or natural causes but solely our intolerable sins." Since Pombal saw in this writing a derogatory reference to his own person, he had the work

confiscated and exiled Father Malagrida to Setúbal. Carvalho "did not lose sight again of the Jesuits, whom he considered the very soul of opposition." Meanwhile Malagrida,
in consequence of his age and the dreadful sufferings and
punishments which he underwent in the long prison years,
seemed to have lost his reason, which caused him at times
to write and do things characteristic of an alienated mind.
The unfortunate old man was condemned by judges, who
were intimidated by Carvalho, to be strangled by the exe-
cutioner and burned on the public square of Lisbon. The
execution took place on July 1, 1761. "For the delight of his
hardened heart," writes Fortunato de Almeida, "the Marquis of Pombal presided at the solemnity. Facing him were
the Monarch and the Court." The Archbishop of Sparta,
who undressed him of the sacred vestments in order to de-
grade him canonically of his religious dignity, exhorted
"piously the accused to confess his crimes and to beg the
King and the people pardon for his felonies." The Jesuit
answered with serene dignity: "Ever since I put my feet on
Portuguese soil, I have always served His Faithful Majesty
as a good and loyal subject; yet if, without knowing, I have
done anything to offend him, I humbly and sincerely ask his
forgiveness." It was one hour past midnight. When the cord
was passed around the martyr's neck to strangle him he
was not frightened. He serenely repeated the words of the
Divine Martyr: "My God, into your hands I deliver my
spirit." At a dinner at the Palace of the Inquisition, Carvalho celebrated the triumph the Catholic faith had obtained that night over the "Jesuitical wickedness."

4. *The Company of Wines of the Upper Douro.* In
September 1756, Carvalho created the Company of Wines
of the Upper Douro with the objective of serving as an
intermediary between the producer and the exporter. But
it also had the objective of breaking the monopoly of wine
exports which the British held. Portuguese interests complained, as did the British, and there was an armed revolt
of the people in Porto. The rebels, however, were subju-
gated, imprisoned, and executed with revolting brutality.
The Jesuits were also involved in the accusation, but they
did not directly participate, either as authors or instigators
of the movement. Nevertheless they were calumniated be-

cause they were charged with the crime of having said that the wines of the Society were not capable of being used in the sacrifice of the Mass.

5. *The Grão-Pará.* Donha Maria, the pious Queen Mother, insisted that the Jesuit missionaries who left for Maranhão relate to her faithfully everything that went on in these missions, even faults and arbitrary deeds committed by the royal officers, promising to keep it secret. Naturally, grave complaints reached the sovereign's ears against Francisco Xavier Mendonça Furtado, Carvalho's brother on his mother's side, and the Queen tried to correct those wrongs through her son. Carvalho, criminally intercepting the letters and violating the Queen's correspondence, easily discovered the origin of the denunciations against his brother. In 1751 Mendonça Furtado traveled to Pará, having been nominated its governor. He carried "Public and Secret Instructions" which gave him freedom to visit the lands of the religious, "notwithstanding any privilege, order, or resolution to the contrary, because I derogate them all, as if I had made express reference to each."

Further still, Mendonça Furtado brought instructions from his brother, the Minister, to take the greatest possible number of priests from the missions and, with the exception of seven or eight for the College of Pará and the same number for the College of Maranhão, to dismiss the rest as being superfluous. Of the Jesuits falsely accused by the governor, three were put on board ship in that year of 1751. The two Portuguese, Teodoro da Cruz and Antônio José, were incarcerated, while the Austrian Rochus Hunderpfund obtained permission from the King to return to his country, despite Carvalho's displeasure at this.[2] These three priests were soon followed by two more. Forgetful of the favors he had previously received from the Jesuits, the Bishop of Pará, Miguel de Bulhões, became a flexible instrument to the new governor and a docile collaborator in the fight against the missionaries of the Society.

Intent on dealing a more definite blow against the missions, Carvalho, with one stroke of the pen, declared the

---

[2] The expulsion of these Jesuits took place in 1755 [ed.].

Indians of Brazil to be free, and extinguished the missions. The Jesuits in Lisbon showed great concern at this act. Father José Moreira, the King's confessor, attempted to talk to him about the matter. Joseph I, however, stopped by Pombal, refused to hear him. Furtado's memoranda relative to the contrary attitude of the Fathers arrived from Pará, and the Jesuit confessors of persons of the royal family were discharged from Court.

6. *Frustrated Marriage.* The Jesuit historian Father Júlio Cordara, in his *Commentaries* about the suppression of the Society of Jesus, adds one more reason which would have particularly set Carvalho against the Jesuits. It was the fact that Father Moreira, the King's confessor, was able to prevent the marriage of Princess Maria Francisca, eldest daughter of Joseph I—a marriage sought by various princes —with Pombal's favorite candidate, the heretical William Henry, son of the King of England. This prince, the Duke of Cumberland, held the rank of Venerable among the English Freemasons.

7. *The Attempted Assassination of King Joseph I.* Another opportunity, well exploited by Carvalho, was the attempted assassination of Joseph I during the night of September 3, 1758. The real cause as well as the real instigators of the crime were never known by the public. The attempt, nevertheless, furnished the Minister with excellent material of accusation cleverly to eliminate several of his personal enemies, all of them of the highest nobility. A long and tiring process of investigation was started in which everything but justice was found. On December 13 the Marquises of Távora, the Duke of Aveiro, and other noblemen related to them, who felt themselves secure at Court, were imprisoned by surprise and accused of trying to rid themselves of the King by ambushing him. The process followed the course set by the Minister, not lacking references to the Jesuits, even to the confession of the Duke of Aveiro which involved the denunciation that four Fathers had agreed to the terrible attempt. Being extremely jealous and affected by popular gossip, the Minister was convinced that there was a vast conspiracy which had armed the hands of the noblemen and which the Jesuits had instigated. There are no traces of positive facts upon which to base

the belief that the Távoras and the Duke of Aveiro were the instruments of the conspiracy.

The Duke said such things, or rather his judges trapped him into saying them, that on January 12, 1759, the sentence was passed with a rigor without precedent: The Marquise of Távora would be decapitated, the Marquis and the Duke would be rolled alive (that is, they would be churned upon a wheel with blows of a club); the Count of Atouguia, José Maria, and the Marquis of Távora, sons of the first, and four servants would also die on the scaffold. The terrible execution took place in Belém on the following morning, and by the savageness of the tortures, by the number of culprits, and by their importance was one of the most abominable spectacles of that period. In this the King identified himself with his Minister: he made him Count of Oeiras. As for the Jesuits, they were not listened to and were unable to defend themselves since Carvalho "abhorred them so much and employed all means to ruin them," as the Count of Merle, French Minister in Lisbon, informed Choiseul. Not being satisfied with the killings of January thirteenth, Carvalho discharged his anger upon the Jesuits, taking advantage of the perplexity and horror caused by the punishment of the Távoras to expel them.

Only six days afterward, on January 19, the mobile and immobile property of the Jesuits of Lisbon as well as their interests and pensions were sequestered. It was a general assault on the houses of the Society. Everything was turned upside down and rummaged, everything was taken and carried away, and a good part of the loot was even sold. Since nothing valuable was found in the residence of the Jesuit Procurators of the Ultramarine missions, the Count of Oeiras sent the six Father Procurators to the dungeons of São Julião.

Simultaneous with the sequestration, royal letters were sent to all the prelates of the kingdom recommending them to warn the faithful against the "impious and seditious errors" of the Jesuits. These orders included the prescription to capture all the spiritual coadjutores (non-professi) and temporal coadjutores (lay brothers) that they might have at hand. "These orders," writes Almeida, "were executed in some parts with extreme barbarity."

Only after three months did the Count of Oeiras propose to inform the Holy See of his acts against the Society of Jesus. Obviously, it was all done in his own manner, written in his emphatic, hard-to-digest style which characterizes all the official documents of that period, and filled with exaggerations, lies, calumnies, and insolences. Helped by his untiring ambassador to the Vatican, Francisco de Almada, by bribery and valuables which he had taken from the houses of the Society, Carvalho had been preparing a favorable climate for his plans in the high circles of the Roman Curia. He intended to disorient Pope Clement XIII and counterbalance any future defense of the Jesuits.

The Holy Father, not wishing to appear partial in this delicate question, tried to satisfy the impertinent demands of the Portuguese government on some points by permitting, for example, the Table of Conscience and Orders of Lisbon to release to the secular curia those Jesuits who had been convicted for participating in the attempt of September third. Yet His Holiness appealed to the King's heart to show clemency toward the accused priests. Carvalho was revolted with the little that the Roman pontiff conceded to him and decided to wield the final blow upon the sons of Loyola with the following law, signed by the monarch on September 3, 1759, the first anniversary of the alleged murder attempt against Joseph I: "After having heard the opinions of many wise and pious ministers, full of zeal for the honor of God, I declare the above-mentioned religious [of the Society of Jesus] to be corrupted, deplorably alienated from their saintly institute, and manifestly indisposed by so many, so abominable, so inveterate, and so incorrigible vices, etc." He threatened capital punishment for any Jesuit who, under any pretext whatsoever, dared to remain within the limits of the outer boundaries of the Portuguese kingdom. He likewise threatened with equal punishment whoever might receive one sole Jesuit or deal with them. Menéndez y Pelayo does not exaggerate when he says that the "story of the expulsion of the Jesuits from Portugal seems like the story of a cannibal feast."

The expulsion was executed without delay throughout the kingdom with inhumanity and even with disrespect for the religious dignity of the exiles.

12

Visconde de Carnaxide

FINANCIAL TROUBLES WERE THE REASON WHY . . .

❖❖❖❖❖❖❖❖❖❖❖❖

*It would not have been surprising to find the expulsion
of the Jesuits explained by a simple reference to economic factors in a work by a Marxist historian. The
Viscount of Carnaxide, a Portuguese aristocrat living
in Brazil until his recent death, seems to have been far
from being that, however. His arguments deserve attention, even if further research might make possible a
more convincing and more modified statement as to
the role of these financial considerations for the action of Pombal.*

Brazil's exports went up tremendously from 1710 to
1760. In 1710 they mounted to a total of £2,500,000
per year. In 1750, when Sebastião de Carvalho ascended to
power, they exceeded £4,000,000. In 1760 they reached
around £5,000,000 sterling. In the sixteen years spanning
1760 and 1776, in the second part of the Pombal administra-

Translated from Visconde de Carnaxide (Antonio de Sousa
Pedroso Carnaxide), *O Brasil na administração pombalina* (São
Paulo, 1940); excerpts from pp. 81-88, 160-161. By permission
of Companhia Editora Nacional, São Paulo.

tion, the most rapid decline registered in the colonial period took place: from close to £5,000,000 exports dropped to £3,000,000. In 1776 exports remained stable. Immediately afterward they rose again uninterruptedly until 1822, up to independence. Consequently, during his first ten years in office, the Minister became used to the fact that all figures from Brazil would rise and rise. But then the star changed. In the following sixteen years the opposite occurred. Everything went down, nothing less than 40 per cent in round numbers. This trend is shown by the graph published by Roberto Simonsen, in which an ascending and a descending line form an acute angle, the vertex of which corresponds to the year 1760.

The magnitude of the crisis (40 per cent), its rapidity (sixteen years), and its perfect synchronization with the last period of the reign of Joseph I together are one of the main causes of the drama that put an end to the feast of Pombal's administration.

The whole nation was hit, little by little, by the crisis of Brazil. Money was spent for the indispensable. Less and less was bought so that commerce and industry became weaker every day. Here is the reason for the failure of all of Pombal's enterprises.

The industries, which should have brought new wealth and which should have become the basis of the new national economy, cost the state larger subsidies each year.

Public expenses went up madly. They went up because of the extraordinary events that occurred during this reign, referred to farther on, and because such an administration could not be economical, dedicated as it was to the acceleration of the material progress of the country and to the realization of daring enterprises. Where could it go for money? Taxes? Loans? Yes, taxes were raised constantly. They were raised to the maximum. . . . But the raising of taxes did not bring a corresponding increase in public revenues. It barely stopped them from being reduced. It compensated for the diminishing of other incomes, nothing more. Also . . . the public debt [was] enlarged to the uttermost limits. It was not always possible, however, to find someone who would make a loan. By 1759 the King was without credit. . . . What could be done? Surrounded by difficulties, the Minister started to make use of expediency. . . .

At the close of the 1750's the Royal Treasury was in great difficulty. The fight against the missions of Uruguay, by then terminated, had cost a fabulous sum. To support this campaign it had been necessary to borrow money and have recourse to the "overdue debts" to a point where the King lost all credit. The work of reconstructing Lisbon, demolished by the earthquake of 1755, lagged. The appropriation destined for this purpose had gone partly to pay creditors of the state and partly for the installation and maintenance of workshops. It was at this time of great financial difficulties that the attempted assassination of King Joseph occurred. The confiscation of the property of the nobles who were executed or imprisoned was "a great help." The Duke of Aveiro was the owner of the largest private fortune in Portugal. Among the others, there were some who had important estates of their own. After the confiscation of the properties of the nobles came that of the Society of Jesus, which was famed for possessing incalculable wealth. It seems beyond doubt that in the persecution of the Society of Jesus the "satanic smile of the economic factor" appeared. Let us examine how the facts occurred.

After the attempt against King Joseph's life, whose authorship was in part attributed to the Jesuits, the confiscation of all the property the Jesuits possessed was ordered. The royal letter of January 19, 1759, charging the Chancellor of the House of Supplication to apply the measures confesses that the sequestration was applied "not by way of jurisdiction, but solely of indispensable economy, and of natural and necessary defense of my royal person, government, and of the public tranquillity of my reign and vassals." Therefore, the basic piece in the process of the confiscation of the order, the royal letter of January 19, 1759, not only mentions the economic factor, but even puts it before the defense of the sovereign, of the government, and of public tranquillity.

The law of September 3, 1759, expelled the Jesuits from the "reigns and domains so that they may not enter again." It should be noted that it expelled them seven months after the royal letter quoted above had been sent, which is to say seven months after their fortune had been taken. It is obvious that if the opposite had been done, the financial result of the operation would have been lost. Nevertheless, if the case of the pretended instigators of the frustrated assassination of the King had been a simple case for the police or of public security, as it is said today, it would have been natural to urgently turn to expelling the Jesuits from the kingdom rather than to retain their property.

The proverb says: The rings go, let the fingers remain. Only this time the government was faster in securing the rings than in procuring the security of the fingers.

The property taken from the Jesuits should be returned to them. Either the property or the profits thereof should be returned to the owners. The return could only be processed through the Papal Court of Rome. King Joseph consulted, or pretended to consult, the Pope in this regard. In the royal letters directed to the chancelors of the houses of supplication of Lisbon and Porto on January 19, 1759, the sovereign stated that he would attempt an understanding with the Apostolic See regarding the movable property and real estate, profits, etc., which on that date he had ordered sequestered and rented in the public square. Also in the letter sent to the Cardinal Patriarch on September 6, 1759, Joseph said: "It will be very much in the service of God, and to my royal pleasure, that you nominate the persons that seem worthy to you to take care of the same churches and edifices of the Society of Jesus, receiving by inventory all the ornaments and furniture of the altars and sacristies of the same churches, and taking care of the conservation of the edifices next to them in order to guard everything with extreme care, while I turn to the Pope so that His Sanctity might determine the use that is to be made of these same churches, furniture, and edifices."

On June 14, 1760, the Portuguese government, taking advantage of a meaningless pretext (the fact that the Apostolic Nuncio did not hang lanterns in his house on the day of the wedding of the Princess of Brazil) ordered the Nuncio to leave "this kingdom immediately, within exactly four days," and cut diplomatic relations with the Apostolic See. Various measures were adopted in connection with the rupture of relations with the Curia. A decree of August 4, 1760, prohibited all persons and secular, ecclesiastical, or regular communities to send money to the Papal Court of Rome "in coin, gold or silver . . . or by means of letters of credit, either sent directly to Rome, to lands of the Pope, or other places in such a way that they will end in Rome or in said lands."

The Count of Oeiras was anxious to put the spoils of the Jesuits legally at the disposal of his insatiable statism. The properties, while they remained only sequestered, were untouchable and were not of much use to him. It was necessary for the Treasury legally to take possession of the properties. King Joseph, pious, fearful, and honorable, was reluctant to lay hands on the belongings of his old educators, confessors, and friends. The process had to be slow. The monarch started to sign documents that tied his hands. Finally, closed in on all sides and faced with the impossibility of the sequestered wealth being sent to Rome, he ordered in a decree of February 25, 1761, that the property of the Jesuits "be immediately incorporated into my Fisc and Royal Chamber and set down on the books of the Property of my Treasury."

The decree of February 25, 1761, arrived in Rio de Janeiro accompanied by the royal letter of October 17 of the same year. This decree ordered the Governor, the Count of Bobadela, to sell in a public sale the buildings and the movable property of the Society "which are not immediately dedicated to worship"; to collect in five years' time the money the Jesuits had lent at an interest; and whatever is received be immediately "remitted on all occasions when ships of war depart."

Let us now return to the beginning and look at an event that merits special attention. The seizure of the property which the sons of Saint Ignatius possessed in Brazil was initially entrusted to the Chief Judge Barberino and two other magistrates. To carry out the mission, these three individuals left Lisbon in 1758. They arrived in Bahia on August 28 and immediately started to execute their mandate. The attempt against Joseph I was on September 3, six days after the arrival of the magistrates. As a result, the persecution of the Society of Jesus did not have, obviously could not have had, the attempt of the King's murder as a determinating cause, although this is the basis on which various legal documents justify it. The persecution of the Society of Jesus, at least in regard to its property, was already decreed, and in part executed, when the attempted murder occurred on September 3, 1758. . . .

The spoils of the sequestration amounted to much less than had been expected. In a dispatch dated April 14, 1769, the Count of Oeiras warned the Marquis of Lavradio, who had just assumed the post of Viceroy of Brazil: "Different are the known enemies from those who are dissimulated. Against these Your Excellency must always be on guard, and always be vigilantly prepared. The first of these are the Jesuits. . . . The second said enemies are the English. . . . All the politics and all the malice of the Jesuits are making the greatest efforts to win the English for their side and to make them take up arms against us. They have publicly transferred to the Banks and Companies of London the most important treasuries which for so many years they extracted from the domains of Portugal and Spain." It was then 1769. The sequestration had been ordered in 1759. Ten years had already gone by. Oeiras did not lose sight of the Jesuits' money which had escaped him. . . .

Carvalho had a great desire for the treasury of the Jesuits. He expected that in this would be the solution to the problems which afflicted him. The smallest public expenses, such as those of the royal carriages, were dependent on that mine. The Ambassador of France, the Count of Merle, in a memorandum to the Duke of Choiseul dated October 16, 1759, referring to our finances, states:

Such was the situation that His Highness, King Joseph, not having the money to undertake the trip to Vila Viçosa, had to use that which had resulted from the sale of possessions and objects belonging to the Jesuits.

What moved Pombal directly against the Jesuits is far from being a question of principle. At a certain point it degenerated into a whim, a *mania*, as Saint-Priest wrote. . . . Originally it had been a question of *means*.

The Expulsion of the Jesuits
from Spanish America

13

Ludwig Von Pastor

A MOST SECRET PROCEDURE

With all due respect to the historians of France, England, the United States, and other countries, it may be maintained that history as a discipline was born in Germany. In the wake of Leopold von Ranke, numerous German scholars of the nineteenth century set out to seek the historical truth with a painstaking use of heuristic analyses, footnotes, and cautious formulations. The great historian of the papacy, Ludwig Pastor, Freiherr von Camperfelden, Professor at the University of Innsbruck and Austrian Minister to the Vatican (1852-1928), belongs to this venerable school. Although he did not conceal his deeply Catholic convictions, his work was by no means an apology. It was the result of diligent and systematic research which revealed the baseness as well as the greatness of the history of the Vatican. The Jesuit order is, of course, an important protagonist in the gigantic work, and Pastor's treatment of the fall of the Jesuits has not been surpassed. The breadth of his exposition makes it difficult to excerpt a few pages. Nevertheless, this sample should give an idea of how the chain of events

From Ludwig von Pastor, *The History of the Popes from the Close of the Middle Ages*, trans. by E. E. Peeler (St. Louis, Mo., 1950), excerpts from Vol. 37, pp. 62-146. Reprinted with the permission of Routledge & Kegan Paul Ltd., London.

leading up to the expulsion of the Spanish Jesuits may reasonably be reconstructed.

The "Hat and Cloak Riots" occasioned, or afforded the pretext for, the expulsion of the Jesuits from Spain. The Fiscal Campomanes held them responsible for the disturbances, and as a result of his memorandum the Society was expelled from every part of the kingdom.

The reports which adhere most closely to events and are still uninfluenced by party motives contain no hint of the Jesuits being responsible for the uprising. . . . The most important document in this respect is the detailed report submitted by Count Aranda to the Minister of Justice, Roda, on April 9, 1766. As the result of the searching and secret inquiries into the origin, course, and actual state of the tumult which he was instituting on behalf of the Court, he repeatedly stresses that the original intention of the rioters had simply been to slaughter the Minister Squillace on Maundy Thursday and thus to rid the nation of a man who by his machinations was preventing the complaints and petition of the people from reaching the ear of the King. In the course of the disturbances the hatred of the Walloon Guard had also played a part. In conclusion Aranda called attention to the extraordinary large number of inflammatory placards by means of which another class of the population was trying to revive the discontent of the masses and to exploit their original actions for their own ends. . . .

Under date April 21, 1766, the king imparted to the President of the Council of Castile the official order and authority to institute a secret inquiry into the excesses that had taken place in the capital. He was to discover the authors, distributors, and instigators of the rebellious pamphlets that had appeared after March twenty-sixth and which purposed by means of distorted news to render the Government detested, to diminish the prestige of the Crown at home and abroad, and to imperil the peace of the realm. The witnesses were not only to have their names kept secret but were to enjoy the special favor of the King. To ensure that the proceedings were carried out in accordance with the law, the President was to avail himself of the services of the Fiscal Campomanes and another member of the Council. . . . An exceptional court of justice was thus set up and was given the misleading name of the "Extraordinary Council of Castile" in order to qualify all the resolutions of this special court in the face of public opinion with the high moral reputation enjoyed by this supreme judicial, legislative, and administrative body.

At the request of the Government the secular clergy were granted leave by the Vicar General of Toledo, and the regular clergy by the Nuncio Pallavicini, to give evidence before the lay judge. . . . The Government's action had indicated that in the Ministries the clergy were thought to be involved in the insurrection, and this supposition became a certainty when the Fiscal Campomanes rendered his first report on June 8, 1766. . . . Campomanes made the following statement: The misleading of the simple people was a result of the preposterous ideas of the royal authority disseminated by the clergy and was a product of the fanaticism they had been propagating for centuries. The lampoons were the work of privileged persons or of those who had acted on their instructions. . . . It was clear, he continued, that this investigation and the action to be taken as the result of it could not take place with due speed in full council, first on account of the difficulty in assembling unobtrusively, and second on account of the variety of opinions, quite apart from the necessity of entrusting numerous subordinate officials with the drawing up of the protocol. They were compelled, therefore, to set up a special chamber which, furnished with the authority of the regular Council, was to meet in the residence of the President of the Council as and when secrecy demanded.

This was nothing more or less than a demand for a secret, exceptional court with secret judges, secret witnesses, and a secret procedure—a truly fitting creation of the absolutist age. The Nuncio's protest that it was a one-sided action against the clergy only was curtly rejected with the remark that no complaints had been laid against laymen.

The spirit in which the commission set to work was revealed still more clearly in the second report which was rendered by Campomanes in the session of September 11,

1766. The inquiry, he stated, had already made such progress that some idea could be formed of how the people had been incited to revolt. Under the cloak of religion, virtue, even of martyrdom, a movement had been provoked which was particularly dangerous on account of the extraordinary secrecy that surrounded it and its apparent peace and order in the midst of the general disorder. In all the ramifications of these intricate incidents could be discerned the activity of a religious body which even during the present inquiry was seeking, by spreading rumors, to win over the clergy and other bodies and to encourage a general dislike of the Government and its principles of reform. . . . Careful consideration would show that these people had been the sole originators of the past disorders and would continue to be such as long as this body existed within the state. . . .

On what grounds did the Fiscal base his charges against the Society of Jesus? As already shown, in the official and private reports that were made in the first few weeks after the risings there was no reference to any Jesuit participation. . . . Various denunciations were made in the course of the inquiries but apparently led to nothing. Some satirical verses, for instance, were sent by a Hieronymite of Cordova to the Grand Inquisitor, but they were judged by him to have come not from the Jesuits but most probably from their bitterest enemies. . . . A certain Fray Marcos Sanchez claimed to know on hearsay evidence of a Jesuit who had said that an association, with the popular preacher Calatayud as its president, had been formed in Pamplona with the object of murdering the King. . . .

When inquiries made in this direction had failed to produce any really suitable grounds for a charge, the Fiscal exerted himself still more energetically to prove by indirect means that the Jesuits had originated the revolt. In one denunciation the Jesuits Martinez and Arnal were accused of having introduced and circulated French apologetic works in Spain without official permission. It is a known fact that at that period Spain was flooded with pamphlets, mostly from France and Portugal, directed not only against the honor of the Society but also against the honor of the King and the monarchy. . . . The Spanish

Jesuits, in their desire to obtain a hearing for the defense against these attacks, had in fact been sending for a year past for apologetic works from abroad and had distributed them in Spanish territory, either in the original text or in Spanish translations. By dint of rumors and ill-will the charge against the Jesuits was aggravated into one of maintaining secret printing presses by means of which the numerous lampoons against the Government had also been produced. . . .

Calatayud, an aged priest, had been giving missions to the people in forty-one dioceses during the previous forty years. In his book *Doctrinas prácticas* and in his sermons he had attacked a form of contract much in vogue among the merchants of Bilbao and had condemned it as usurious. The merchants complained to Count Aranda, who, with the agreement of the Extraordinary Council, ordered the missionary to leave the Basque provinces at once. Calatayud abandoned the mission he was giving and left the next day for Valladolid. The General of the Order, through his Provincial Idiaquez, instructed his subjects to exercise the greatest care in their sermons and private conversations and above all to refrain from any criticism of the Government. . . .

By the middle of October the secret inquiry was sufficiently advanced for the Fiscal to round off his charge and lay it before the Extraordinary Council. At Aranda's request Charles III granted the Council authority to accept the Fiscal's charge and proposals and to take whatever steps he thought suitable, though he was to obtain the King's decision before the final resolution was taken. . . . In accordance with a . . . decree of October 31, 1766, all the members of the Council were bound by oath to observe the strictest silence about the names of the witnesses and the whole proceedings; any infringement of this prohibition would be regarded as high treason.

These long negotiations being at last concluded, the day of decision drew near which was to seal the fate of the Jesuits in the Spanish world. In the session of January 29, 1767, the Extraordinary Council, adopting the opinion of the Fiscal Campomanes, decided on the banishment of the Jesuits from the realms under the Spanish Crown and on the confiscation of their property by the state. The relative document, which was submitted for the royal approval, was in two parts. The first consisted of a historical description of the facts and the legal grounds on which the court had arrived at its verdicts, the second dealt with the measures by which the resolution was to be put into effect. Unfortunately, the first and more important part has been mislaid, but the gap is filled by a document (*Exposición sumaria*) which, it is true, was compiled by Moñino for Clement XIV two years after the Jesuit expulsion, but which represents in the main an extract from the missing first part of the memorandum of January 29, 1767. The gist of it is as follows.

From the time of Charles III's accession to the throne of Spain the Jesuits had evinced a definite dislike for his person and his Government. Accustomed to the despotism which they had formerly enjoyed as Court confessors, they saw with bitterness that their creatures were no longer promoted to high offices because the King, in his enlightened wisdom, was no longer willing to tolerate the misuse they had made of their power for so many years. Among the various complaints which came to the ears of the monarch were two which grievously affected the body and the government of the Society of Jesus. The churches in India [Spanish America] complained of the unheard-of violence with which the Jesuits had cheated them out of their tithes. Bitter complaints were also brought to the foot of the throne by the postulators for the canonization of Palafox; namely, that through the crafty machinations of the Jesuits . . . some of the works of this venerable servant of God were burnt, to the scandal of the nation. . . . By listening to these representations the King offended the honor and self-interest which had always been the idols of this terrible Society. At the same time, by a happy chance, their usurpation of sovereignty in Paraguay was discovered, and also their rebellion and ingratitude, as was clear from the authentic, original documents, which brought to light the usurpation and the excesses which for a century and a half were a problem, or rather an impenetrable mystery, for the whole world. . . . That the monarch entrusted the instruction of his children to members of this body was a

clear indication that he had no personal dislike of them. But
as the Jesuits were not to be satisfied with anything less
than the recovery of their former arbitrary power, they
formed the plan of setting the whole kingdom in a state of
turmoil, and it was only by the special protection of Prov-
idence that the realm was preserved from the terrors of a
civil war and its disastrous consequences. For a long past
they had sown among the loyally Catholic Spanish people
suspicion both of the King and his Ministers, as though
they were heretics and as though religion had declined
since the King's arrival and would be changed in Spain
within a few years. They spread these and other terrible
slanders at first in private conversation, later in their Exer-
cises, giving their opinion of the Government and its measures in a deprecatory manner. . . . After the Jesuits had
prepared men's minds in this manner for some time, they,
as ringleaders and plotters, held their secret meetings in
the capital, and here that terrible revolt was hatched. At
first, no doubt, it was directed against the Finance Minister,
Squillace, and his ordinances, but the Jesuits were skillful
enough to turn it into a war of religion, the rioters calling
themselves soldiers of the Faith. . . . The disturbances in
Spain were accompanied by news of increased unrest in
America. . . . Their own writings showed that they had
set up an absolute monarchy in Paraguay, or rather an unprecedented despotism hostile to all the laws of God and
man. The revolts of the Indians against Spain and Portugal
owed their origin to the Jesuits and their leadership. In
Chile, according to their own accounts, they encouraged
heathen customs, known as Machitun. In all their American missions their unbounded supremacy in spiritual and
temporal matters was established. . . . In the Philippines
they preached against the Government, and during the occupation of Manila their Provincial contravened the law
and stood on good terms with the English general. . . .
From these general conditions in Spain and its colonies and
from the dangers that threatened, it was clear that there
was absolutely no other remedy for this mass of evils than
for the nation to cast out from her bosom these ferocious
enemies of her tranquility and happiness. . . . Any idea of
reforming the Jesuits was not only useless but highly dan-

gerous. What hope could there be of a reform when this incorrigible body, in spite of its expulsion from France and Portugal, not only did not humble and improve itself but plunged into still greater crimes? The reform that had begun in Portugal at the King's request had brought about a dastardly attempt on his life. What Minister could advise his royal master to risk his valuable life while the reform was in progress? And what monarch could abandon his own safety and that of his realm during this period to the rage of the Jesuits? Moreover, a reform of this utterly depraved body would be tantamount to its destruction. With the Jesuits it was impossible and unnecessary to distinguish between the guilty and the innocent. It was not that every member had been let into the secret of the conspiracy; on the contrary, many had acted in good faith; but these above all were the most dangerous enemies of the monarchy since by reason of their simplicity they were most easily used as tools by their superiors. . . .

On the strength of this indictment by the Fiscal the Extraordinary Council proposed the banishment of the Jesuits, the seizure of their property, and the absolute prohibition of any written correspondence with them. On February 20, 1767, a special commission (*Junta especial*) met to examine this resolution; it was composed of the Ministers Roda, Muniain, Muzquiz, and Grimaldi, together with the Duke of Alba, Masones, and the King's confessor, Osma. In view of the facts and weighty considerations which had been stated, also the integrity, experience, and erudition of the members of the Extraordinary Council, which ruled out any doubt of the thoroughness, justice, and legality of their proceedings, the special commission came to the conclusion that the King could and should make their verdict his own. With regard to the plan for carrying out this verdict the commission proposed seven amendments which amounted to a lessening of the severities attached to the law of banishment, such as that not every case of secret correspondence with the exiles was to be treated as one of high treason. To forestall any discussion about the motives for the banishment, the King was to include in the decree a statement that he was locking away in his royal breast the reasons for this decision, without entering into any judgment of the Institute of the Society of Jesus, or the morals and principles of its members. . . .

"Relying on the memorandum of the Extraordinary Council and of other highly placed persons, moved by weighty reasons, conscious of his duty to uphold obedience, tranquility, and justice among his people, and for other urgent, just, and compelling causes, which he was locking away in his royal breast," Charles III issued on February 27, 1767, the decree whereby he banished from Spain and its possessions overseas all Jesuits who had taken their first vows and novices who refused to secede, and ordered the appropriation of their movable and immovable property. The execution of this order was entrusted to Count Aranda, who was vested with full and exclusive powers. All civil authorities and the Superiors of the Order were required to obey the ordinance promptly under pain of the royal displeasure. . . .

The Jesuits knew, of course, that secret inquiries were afoot and that certain malignant persons intended to use every means to implicate them in the insurrections, but strangely enough they placed their trust in the very persons who were to be the chief authors of their ruin, namely Aranda and the King. It was true that Aranda was a former pupil of theirs, that he had close relatives in the Order, and that his house was frequented by the Jesuit Martinez. And Charles III had recently shown them marks of favor. The Jesuits Zacanini and Wedlingen were still teaching the royal princes, and continued to do so, right to the very eve of banishment. . . . Even as late as January 11, 1767, forty Jesuits sailed from Cádiz to the missions in Paraguay and Chile with the royal assent. In spite of all this, the fear persisted in Madrid and Rome that certain persons were trying to kindle in Spain the same conflagration that had destroyed the Order in France . . . private individuals were spreading out the report in confidential conversations that the extirpation of the Society in Spanish territory had already been decided and that it would soon be put into effect.

These rumors were well founded. On March 1, 1767, the decree of banishment of February twenty-seventh was handed to Aranda who straightway drew up an executive instruction, which he had secretly reproduced, together with the decree and a circular note, in the royal printing press. Separate instructions were sent by the King to his officials, commanding them to carry out faithfully all the orders which Aranda would issue to them in the King's name and to address all correspondence on this matter to Aranda only. To lull the Jesuits into a sense of security and to distract public attention Aranda suspended on March fourth and fifth respectively the prohibitions against the holding of popular missions by Father Calatayud and in the Basque provinces. But the rumors persisted despite these attempts of his to mask his real intentions. . . . Aranda, who had been informed by the political secret service of the rumors that were current, decided that any long delay would be dangerous. . . . The King left it to the President's judgment to fix the final date for the carrying out of the decree. . . . Aranda therefore decided that the decree should come into effect on the night of April 2-3 for the country as a whole and the night of March 31-April 1 for Madrid and its environs. . . .

Ordinances similar to those for the mother country were sent on March 6, 1767, to the Spanish colonies in South America and to the Philippines. In a supplementary instruction of March 1, 1767, the President of the Extraordinary Council invested the Viceroys, Governors, and Presidents overseas with all his own powers and ordered them to convey the missionaries to Puerto de Santa María, near Cádiz, where they would receive further instructions. The civil administration of mission districts was to be entrusted provisionally to men of proved integrity. The spiritual welfare of the missions, which in the future would be under the direct control of the Bishops, was to be handed over to secular priests or to other religious. Missionaries in very remote situations were to be recalled by their Provincial or his representative without further information. To forestall any underhand delays on the part of the Provincial, the arrest of the Jesuits in the colleges was to be carried out first, so that the missionaries to the heathen would obey orders more readily on seeing that they had been deprived of these supports. While observing the necessary security measures, the executive officials were to treat the missionaries, who were expected to submit quite readily, in a respectful and kindly manner and to use force only if unavoidable.

14

Gabriel René-Moreno

TO CARRY OUT THE ORDERS IN THE MOST REMOTE WILDERNESS

❖❖❖❖❖❖❖❖❖❖❖

How the decision of Charles III to expel the Jesuits finally reached the form of a decree and detailed instructions was the subject of the preceding extract. But there was also a long step between the arrival of these orders at the headquarters of colonial administration and their execution, particularly in the mission districts. Nowhere was this step more difficult than in the case of the Mojos missions in Alto Perú, present-day Bolivia.

The result of the expulsion in this area also proved to be extremely important. A Bolivian historian writing in 1939 asserts that the decline in the Bolivian Oriente *has never been stopped, once initiated by the expulsion of the Jesuits.*

The text reproduced here is taken from an account

Translated from *Narraciones históricas* by G. René-Moreno; selection, prologue, and comments by E. Kempff Mercado (Washington, 1952), excerpts from pp. 85-118; printed by permission of the Pan American Union. The other book alluded to is Enrique Finot, *Historia de la Conquista del Oriente Boliviano* (Buenos Aires, 1939), p. 363.

*written by Gabriel René-Moreno (1836-1908), Boliv-
ia's most remarkable historian and one of the pioneers
of historical scholarship in Latin America. He spent
most of his life in Chile, but his whole historical work
was devoted to his* patria. *Combining relatively advanced research techniques and vast bibliographical
knowledge with a powerful prose, René-Moreno did
not publish very much, but what he produced was
solid and thoughtful. While his best-known work is*
Últimos días coloniales en el Alto Perú, *the present
text first appeared in the rather rare* Biblioteca Boliviano. Catálogo del Archivo de Mojos y Chiquitos
(Santiago de Chile, 1888).

Using the necessary secrecy and by means of orders
that were circulated with unheard of rapidity, the
President of Upper Peru had ordered that the expulsion
of the Jesuits in the vast district of the Audiencia of Charcas
should begin at daybreak of September 4, 1767. The simultaneous arrest of all the members and confiscation of all
the properties of the Society were to take place on that
day and hour. From that moment on, no time was to be
lost or effort spared in the removal of the Fathers from
every corner of the land. They were to be sent through
the desert from Oruro to Arica, finally being placed at the
disposal of the Viceroy in Lima.

The orders concerning the Jesuits who ruled the missions
of Mojos and Chiquitos were the most difficult of all to
carry out. This is easily explained.

Those establishments were situated in remote territories which were extensive and almost unknown. The
routes which led there, by land and water, were tortuous.
The proposed sudden and violent *coup* faced greater and
more diverse drawbacks there than in any other part of
the viceroyalty. Those mission Indians had lived for a full
century grateful and submissive to the Fathers. Until this
time they had known no other authority than these representatives of God on earth. They had never felt the touch
or the weight of secular rule. Was it not to be feared that
they might present strong opposition in favor of their

revered guardians, or that they might arise in a furious mob, or that they might flee, terrified, to the mountains and savagery? . . .

Whether prudently calculated by the Court or directly suggested by other events, there was an excellent basis for the execution of the scheme against the Jesuits of Mojos at that time, even though it was the most difficult part of the vast conspiracy of the expulsion. On the banks of the Itenes, facing that clandestine Portuguese stockade Santa Rosa, which was soon to be converted forever into the fort of Beyra, was a body of regular troops from Upper Peru and Santa Cruz. They were the remnants of an expedition which had come there from Cochabamba the preceding year, under the command of President Pestaña, with the apparent desire of dislodging the Portuguese from that bank. Nevertheless, the issue did not come to a battle. The general retired from the field in the face of the enemy, and ordered most of his infantry and all of his artillery to retreat. The Court in Madrid had decreed a suspension of hostilities.

With only the skeleton of the army, Colonel Antonio Aymerich remained there in Pestaña's place fighting the inclemencies of a humid and burning climate, the rigors of a fatal epidemic. The troops were abandoned by the Commissariat of War, which was in the habit of leaving these servants of the King without pay or medications. By the end of the year five hundred men were left buried there without having fired a shot. The survivors waited tenaciously for a second order against the Portuguese to be signed. The orders arrived, against the Jesuits. . . .

On the banks of the deep, swift Itonama, not far from the Portuguese stockade in the extreme north of what is today Bolivia, the troops were quartered in the Magdalena mission. The chief arrived there carrying the close secret of the expulsion without yet having recovered from his surprise.

Reversing his position from then on, all alone, Aymerich could uneasily regard the immeasurable plains of Mojos before him. Spreading out monotonously, without texture, from the banks of the Itenes, the Beni, and an intermediate transverse section of the Mamoré to the north unrolled a surface of 13,750 square leagues, until it touched Yura-carés, the foot of the last spur of the Andes. It spread on to lose itself in the gigantic forests of the south which separated Mojos from the plains of Santa Cruz de la Sierra, a few steps higher and a hundred times more beautiful. . . .

The torrential summer rains converted the peaceful plains into a single immense, navigable sea in all directions, dotted by islands. The islands were the mission towns situated on the high, dry spots, as well as the ranches, small farms, and corrals which occupied a few little hillocks of dry land, but which were not always free from flood. The waters retreated in the river beds and everything dried up outside the rivers; never, however, did the hundred shades of green dry up or go away . . . they persisted in the woods and thickets which encircled and speckled the plains. . . .

It was a tropical region with extreme alternations of sky and soil. The low plain, which received the waters of six months of rain as well as the runoff from the eastern slopes of the ranges and the northern and western slopes of Chiquitos and Mato Grosso, was furrowed by thirty-four rivers which were navigable at any time for almost their entire length. It was split in half, south to north, by the tempestuous Mamoré, with its often sunken, moving, and inconsistent banks. And yet it was all inhabitable by virtue of the wise economy of nature, which made Mojos hot and dry in winter and bathed by interminable rains in summer. Over all this and its population of 18,535 robust, docile neophyte Indians, reigned 23 regulars of the Society of Jesus with exclusive, absolute, and paternal authority, in the year 1767. The Indians, who were outstanding for their native ingenuity, kindness, innocence, liberality, and happiness, were neatly gathered into fifteen towns ranged around magnificent churches.

No one was lazy here; everyone worked; they worked communally under the tutelage of the priests, without individual holdings, without knowing about the use of money or the give and take of business. They received everything from the hands of the priests; from their food and clothing for their families to blessing and religious instruction, from the teaching of crafts and the example in the work to temporal punishment and the examples of Heaven and Hell.

They wove, tanned leather, carved wood, melted and forged metal, sowed, boiled sugar cane, sewed, spun, made shoes, played instruments, sang, cultivated and worked the cacao, and herded the three species of cattle. They produced everything they needed for this rudimentarily civilized life. Furthermore, they produced a variety of desirable articles which were taken from Santa Cruz and sold in Upper Peru under the auspices of the Jesuit agents in La Plata, Potosí, Oruro, Cochabamba, and La Paz.

The purchasing agency of the Lima college received from those of Alto Peru the money from Mojos and Chiquitos, which was needed for the payment of European merchandise, requested by the missions and sent to them from Lima. . . .

The Fathers were the absolute masters of Paila, a commercial port on the Guapay, twelve leagues east of Santa Cruz. The missions of Mojos and Chiquitos used Paila exclusively, for it was their only port of entry. It had warehouses, stockyards for cattle stock brought in by canoe, an adequate stock of mules and carts for the overland transportation between the river and the city. The Jesuits had a college there which provided lodging for the Society and a depot for goods on sale or en route to Upper Peru. Furthermore, this college was a lookout, dogging the steps of the Governor and the Bishop.

Briefly stated, the strict, exaggerated, forceful, and secret orders of the Court were: to fall without warning on the Jesuits, seizing all their properties and papers; to remove them from the land as soon as possible without provoking any kind of conflict; to begin at once an inventory of everything confiscated, worldly as well as ecclesiastic; to act as a rapid, strong, sure, and inexorable arm, blind and impartial even to the sick and the decrepit and crippled ancients, sensible only of the respect due the priestly character of the Jesuits and careful to allay any undue suffering on their trip.

In order to comply with them fully, the President of Charcas sent his own orders to Aymerich personally. He

ordered him to take advantage of the amazement of the
natives by removing the Fathers from Mojos before the
rains, which broke their dikes there a little before November. He prevailed on him to replace all the Jesuits at the
same time, in the fifteen parishes, with priests of both the
regular and secular clergy from Santa Cruz and Upper
Peru, which the Bishop of the diocese would be instructed
to send him in time. He advised him to make the deposi-
tions very cautiously, to evade any withholding of properties or cash, and that he should be very careful to let
the Indians feel this brand-new secular authority with gentle and attractive firmness. . . .

It quickly became obvious that this could not occur as a
simultaneous blow in the early morning of September
fourth. Undoubtedly, that day was poorly chosen with
respect to Mojos. . . .

Meanwhile, toward the end of August, a vague rumor
which descended from the south began to circulate in all
the colleges and rectories of Mojos. It whispered into the
ears of the Jesuits that a secret dispatch, containing something very grave against them from the King, was to be
opened in Santa Cruz on a fixed day, the date of which
they did not know. Immediately the rumor began to
spread, sowing a certain consternation even among the Indians, at the same time that Aymerich's little group, direct-
ing themselves toward the large river, left the waters of
the Machupo entirely in the district of Baures.

The truth is that the secret concerning the expulsion,
which should have been strictly kept, leaked out through
the government of Santa Cruz. Furthermore, according to
contemporary information, it seems that a brief, extremely
reserved notice was circulated from the college of La Plata
in the middle of July, leaving the Jesuits of Upper Peru
and the missions alert and prepared. . . .

But the Jesuits never thought for a moment of obstructing
the swift accomplishment of the sovereign's will. Neither
were anger and the desire for vengeance what this great
blow elicited from the breasts of those good, simple natives. They were destined, after the departure of their
present guardians, to render heroic proofs of gentleness
and patience. Lacking the excellent characteristic of their

jovial disposition, trusting and ready to serve the white man, they might have been shattered and withered in the very depths of their souls by the terror that now seized all of them. The instinctive cry of this race was "flee!" and to flee, for them, meant to return to the mountains and barbarity.

The greatest disturbance was felt in Loreto, Trinidad, and San Pedro, the towns of Mamoré, tied to this central artery by streams and lagoons which could almost always be navigated, then, up to the very hills where each mission stood.

In Loreto the natives began to gather up their women, children, and clothing; not a few left to hide themselves in the forest. It was difficult for the priests of that village to quiet, calm, and recall the terrified number. In Trinidad the curate, in order to contain the people who were unwilling to listen to reason, forced them into the church by a very solemn manner and, mounted in the pulpit, finally succeeded with menacing exhortations and almost superstitious threats to re-establish order. . . .

In view of what happened in Loreto, Trinidad, and San Pedro, the Father Superior sent a message to Aymerich in order to assure him that everything was still tranquil and that from then on he could take less precautions. He also informed him that, if what was being said about the expulsion of the Jesuits were true, then he should know beforehand that the latter would be ready to obey immediately, and that they would continue to follow silently whatever destiny the King's will had presented them. . . .

Aymerich remained calm about this area. It is clear how the good results of this proceeding smoothed the entire task enormously. . . .

On October 4, 1767, after having formally obeyed the royal decree, both Jesuit missionaries in [Loreto] delivered the parish to the provisional priest sent by the Bishop of Santa Cruz. In the meantime Aymerich's commissioners began the deposition of the local properties, and made the corresponding inventories. By dawn the notice of the order of general expulsion had left Mojos for the Superior of these missions in San Pedro.

The wording was respectful, but, by force of events,

peremptory, absolute, hard, and military. Thus, without a moment's loss a message should be sent by the Superior to all the colleges and rectories, so that the distant missionaries should be ready to leave at the first notice, and so they might prepare in the meantime for a punctual delivery of their goods, inventoried and sworn to; it further stated that no one, of whatever rank, should be excused from delivering himself in Loreto.

One after another of the exiles were disembarked not far from San Carlos in Jorés, on the banks of a tributary of Rio Grande or Guapay, which is a tributary of the Mamoré. From there they proceeded overland on horseback. Aymerich gave very strict orders that a poor old man, painfully ill, should be carried in a hammock. The governor of Santa Cruz had moved to Buenavista in order to be in sight of what he called "the ousting of the Jesuits." The escorts from Mojos delivered the exiles to the care of the city escort in Jorés. The first party of five Fathers spent no less than twenty-four days traveling from Loreto to this city. . . .

The upper classes were no better informed in the matter than the lower with their fantastic and confused notions. Before the first notices concerning the expulsion were received from Aymerich, the ideas improvised by the Court concerning the legal condition in which the natives were to be left prevailed among the President, the Attorney for Native Affairs, and the judges of the Audiencia in Chuquisaca. . . .

It was proposed that the lands be distributed among the families so that on this fixed base individual capital might be quickly substituted for the existing communism.

It would be necessary to dictate and elaborate, immediately, temporal and spiritual laws in the viceroyalty which would take these neophytes by the hand and gently put them under the ordinary rule of the colonial regime for natives. Mojos needed a political governor, a society of landowning subjects, a neighborhood of responsible freemen, tax collectors designated for the towns, everything just as it was in the hamlets and districts of the Upper Peruvian Indians. . . .

A few documents bearing exact dates and figures concerning Mojos had been discovered in the Upper Peruvian purchasing agencies. The President and his counselors were understood to have acquired a basic knowledge of most of their business from these.

According to them, a province where 54,345 head of cattle and 26,371 horses grazed on the green area comprised between 66 square Castilian leagues, south to north, and 102 for east to west; a province in the temples of which one could find at this instant a hoard of 19,000 marks of worked silver, not counting 630 ornaments of silk tissue and brocade, or those of gold and precious stones, or paintings and artistic sculptures, or furniture, or portraits, beautifully carved; a province which exported, in seed and in fruit, the entire crop from its cacao orchards, a great variety of artifacts, and a surplus from the yearly income from its ranches and farms; . . . such a province could learn to live nicely without tutors. Without any doubt, it would have the resources with which to sustain both its spiritual and its temporal ministers, self-sufficient in the means to supply its further economic and political life equally with the rest of the kingdom.

Thus said, they resolved it so; and to verify the proverb which says that little things signal larger ones, in those days the judges bought in Chuquisaca a few enormous volumes, costly and weighty as bricks, which they sent to the Governor of Mojos so that, on this foundation, he might build the secular and antitheocratic structure of the new province. These bricks were the Laws of the Indies and the Ordinances of Viceroy Toledo. Even so, by reason of stronger forces, they were destined never to reign in Mojos; not for a day, an hour, or a second.

15

Herbert Ingram Priestley

THE OPPOSITION QUELLED
IN BLOOD

◇◇◇◇◇◇◇◇◇◇◇◇

*The most famous among the executors of Charles
III's expulsion decree was José de Gálvez, at the time
Visitor-General in New Spain, later to become Secretary of Overseas Affairs. His best biographer is Herbert I. Priestley, born in 1875 and a long-time teacher of
Latin-American history at the University of California
at Berkeley. He succeeded Herbert Bolton as Director
of the Bancroft Library. Priestley's literary style is un-
distinguished, but his scholarship is sound. This excerpt covers the only immediate political consequence
of the expulsion of the Jesuits from Spanish America.
These disturbances in northern Mexico have sometimes been described in an exaggerated way, or, on the
contrary, they have been ignored by the writers on
the fall of the order.*

From Herbert I. Priestley, *José de Gálvez, Visitor-General of
New Spain, 1765-1771* (Berkeley, Calif., 1916), excerpts from
pp. 211-229. Reprinted by permission of the University of California Press.

The order for the expulsion reached Croix on May 30.
He had been viceroy for just nine months, hardly time
to establish himself in his office in a land where the movement of political life and administration was extremely
slow. He had learned, however, that the power of the
Jesuits with the people of New Spain was very great, and it
was feared that the execution of the royal order would be
accompanied by grave disorders. He had good reason to
believe that the Society was anticipating hostile action on
the part of the government, as sufficient time had elapsed
since the expulsion from Spain in March[1] for the leaders of
the Jesuits in New Spain to be apprised of that action. He
also suspected that the Society might take measures to resist the accomplishment of the plans of the Crown against
them. Accordingly he confided his plans for the stroke to
no one save Gálvez and his own nephew, Teodoro de
Croix. The account of the preparations for and the execution of the order is best given in the words of Croix himself:

> As all the inhabitants are worthy pupils and zealous
> partisans of that Company . . . I took good care to
> trust none of them with the execution of the orders
> of the King. The secret would surely have got out,
> which would by no means have been convenient. For
> this reason it was that I decided to confide in none save
> the Señor de Gálvez, a minister who is employed here
> in the King's service, and in your son; we three, there-
> fore, made all the arrangements ourselves, writing
> with our own hands all the orders necessary; these
> were immediately dispatched by special messengers,
> that they might be carried out simultaneously in the
> most remote places of this vast empire.
>
> Until now the business has had the best success; nei-
> ther the troops nor any member of the public discov-
> ered the secret until daybreak of the twenty-fifth of
> the present month [June], which was the date I had se-

---

[1] Although the expulsion took place in Madrid on the night
of March 31, in the rest of the country the day chosen was
April 2 [ed.].

lected for the promulgation of the sentence. It was executed at the same hour in all the colleges and other houses of the Company, whose money, goods, and general effects were at the same time sequestered to the King.

Effort is now being made, while orders are being awaited, to arrange everything so that no one may be injured. The secret was so well kept that the entire public is not yet recovered from the extreme surprise it experienced at the outset, a circumstance which— added to the fact that the troops were under arms— has contributed not a little to the marked tranquility with which everything has passed off, as well here as in the principal cities around about. These are the only places of which I can at present write you, as I have not yet been able to obtain news from those which are at greater distance. Nevertheless, as the orders were uniform, I flatter myself that the results must have been the same. . . .

Gálvez says, concerning preparation for the execution of the order, that the greatest care was exercised in the choice of officers sent to the outlying provinces for that purpose. . . .

While there had been no disturbances in Mexico and Puebla during the expulsion, there had been riots in the mining regions, of which Croix was not informed when he wrote the letter above quoted. To the north, in San Luis de la Paz, San Luis Potosí, and Guanajuato, where trouble with the lower classes was chronic, the expulsion had failed of execution. There were also riots and insurrections in Valladolid and Pátzcuaro. Many of these disorders were due to the renewal of orders against carrying arms, to the collection of the tribute, undertaken at this time with renewed vigor, and to the collection of excises on "regional beverages." When Croix was about to send a minister of the Audiencia to quell these disturbances, Gálvez offered to go himself, "after filling the heart of the gentle viceroy with suspicion as to the true cause of the commotions," that is, after making him believe that they were due to the expulsion, and not to economic discontent. . . .

He set out from Mexico on July 9, 1767, vested with the full powers of the Viceroy, in the same form as he was later to be authorized to act for Croix while on the California and Sonora expedition. He was preceded on July 5 and 7 by three detachments of the troops which had guarded the expulsion from Mexico and Puebla. . . . The first objective point of Gálvez was San Luis de la Paz, which is northeast of Guanajuato, near the eastern boundary of the modern state of that name. The commissioners of the expulsion had been driven out of San Luis de la Paz on June 25, without having executed their orders. Again, on the night of the seventh of July, riots occurred when the *alcalde mayor* attempted to take the Jesuits from their college. When they heard of the approach of Gálvez with troops, the Fathers fled while he was yet two days distant: this was about the middle of July. The leaders of the riots were caught and given summary trials by the Visitor, who sat as a military judge, in his capacity as intendant of the army. On July 20 four ringleaders of the tumults were executed, two others being whipped and exiled. In San Luis de la Paz, Gálvez obtained possession of certain seditious circulars of unknown origin, which had been distributed for the purpose of urging defiance to the King's order of expulsion. Three months later a Franciscan minorite confessed to the authorship of the circulars; he was sent to Mexico to prison. . . .

On the next to the last day of his stay at San Luis de la Paz, Gálvez received three urgent appeals for help from San Luis Potosí. At that place the *alcalde mayor*, who was being assisted in attempts to effect the expulsion by Francisco Mora, a rich Creole farmer, was having serious trouble with the Indians of the town and of the mines. Gálvez therefore dispatched a troop of cavalry thither, and ordered a cordon thrown about the Cerro de San Pedro, the hilly region in which the mines of the district were located. He then set out from San Luis de la Paz on July 21, reaching Potosí on the morning of the twenty-fourth. Here the Jesuits were still in their church. Deploying his forces upon all the streets of the place, Gálvez advanced upon the church, where a huge crowd was collected. He ordered the people out, closed the doors, ascended to the rector's room, and curtly ordered the Fathers brought from their rooms and taken to the street under guard, allowing time only for coaches to be prepared and a few garments collected. The Jesuits were taken away under guard of seventy dragoons, who conducted them to the limits of the province, where they were met and escorted to Vera Cruz by a sergeant from Jalapa with twelve men. The rector of the church was expelled along with the other Jesuits, contrary to the usual practice observed during the expulsion, as he was believed by Gálvez to have been responsible for many of the recent disturbances which had occurred among the mining population. Especially was this measure deemed advisable since it was rumored on all sides that a general massacre of the Spaniards had been planned for St. James' Day, July 26, two days later than the date of Gálvez' arrival. All the shops had been closed and the Spanish population had taken refuge in the convents. The plan of the insurgents included setting up an independent government and the readoption of the native religion. . . .

Once the Jesuits were gone, Gálvez ordered the shops to reopen and the people to return home from their refuges in the convents. Summary trials of the rioters began at once. On August 7 eleven of them were sentenced to be hung and their heads set on pikes until time should consume them. Their homes were ordered destroyed and the sites strewn with salt. Thirty-nine other unfortunates were sent to prison for life and five more were exiled. In a neighboring village, San Nicolás, eleven persons were condemned to death: the leader of the revolt was condemned to be quartered and exposed on pikes for having sworn not to lay down arms until he had done away with the *Gachupines* [Spaniards]. The hand of the secretary who had written the oath was cut off and similarly exposed; the village was deprived of all local autonomy until that should be restored by royal clemency, as the whole town was adjudged accessory to the revolt.

In Guadalcázar four more persons were condemned to death. Here the rebels had forced from the authorities a humiliating capitulation, signed publicly in the plaza, in which it was specified that the government monopolies of revenues and the *alcabala* should be abolished, and an Indian or a Creole recognized as king. . . .

At San Francisco, ten leagues from Potosí, the Indians had been encouraged to revolt by a Jesuit who was acting as parish priest. The cause of disaffection was the organization of militia and the consequent collection of taxes. The priest Gálvez turned over to the bishop of Michoacán for punishment. The bishop exculpated the Jesuit on the score of insanity, but Gálvez sent him to Mexico, with the recommendation that he be sent to Spain for trial. Eight natives were executed for sedition, two were sentenced to the lash and banishment, seven went to prison for life, and twenty-six for limited terms. . . .

Viewed in the light of twentieth-century standards, the severity of Gálvez while upon this expedition can hardly be considered a cause for inner satisfaction or consolation. It is difficult to refrain from the judgment that his sentences were heartlessly cruel. During the trials no actual destruction of life was proved to have been committed by the turbulent natives, though some attempts at such violence had been made. Much property had been destroyed and a decidedly anti-Spanish spirit had been uncovered. Of 3,000 persons brought to trial, all had been found "to have hearts full of malice and a desire to do the Spaniards mischief." By the standards of today, these would be considered light offenses for the punishments inflicted. Eighty-five men had gone to death, seventy-three to the lash, six hundred seventy-four had been condemned to term or life imprisonment, and one hundred seventeen to banishment. We can have no knowledge of the number of women and children who were deprived of support by these sentences. "But I assure you before God, and with all sincerity," wrote Gálvez, "that I have not upon my conscience the slightest scruple of having exceeded the limits of justice, for I mitigated my sentences always with clemency and mercy." Perhaps if this statement had been strictly true, Gálvez would not have felt impelled to utter it with such vehemence. Men rarely hurry to the defense of their consciences unless these have been challenged from within. One would like to know what one Miguel Hidalgo y Costilla, a youth of fourteen summers when Gálvez came to his city of Valladolid, thought of the justice of the visitor-general. There was also Morelos, a child of only two short years, but even he may have remembered what he must then have seen. The generation which was to begin the revolutionary movement was old enough to have some recollection, if not to feel strongly the influence, of the personality of the militant reformer of New Spain.

16

Julio César González

AN EXECUTOR WHO WAS BETTER THAN HIS FAME

◇◇◇◇◇◇◇◇◇◇◇◇◇

Nowhere did the expulsion of the Jesuits seem to form a more formidable task than in the Province of Río de la Plata, of which the famous Guaraní missions formed a part. Would the Jesuits and the Indians disobey the expulsion orders and another "Guaraní War" take place? The mission area had a population of about 73,000 by then—and even more, rumor had it.

The execution of the order was entrusted to Governor Francisco de Paula Bucareli y Ursúa (whose brother later became a famous Viceroy of New Spain). He has usually been described as both cruel and inept in carrying out his task. A Jesuit historian, Father Pablo Hernández, has been particularly active in spreading this view. According to him, the dispatch of the two Bucareli brothers to America was also part of the anti-Jesuit conspiracy in Madrid because

Translated from Julio César González, "Notas para una historia de los treinta pueblos de Misiones. El proceso de la expulsión de los jesuítas (1768)," *Anuario de Historia Argentina (1942)* (Buenos Aires, 1943); excerpts from pp. 274-343. His polemic remarks refer to the introduction to Pablo Hernández, *El extrañamiento de los jesuítas del Río de la Plata y de las Misiones del Paraguay por decreto de Carlos III* (Madrid, 1908).

both were hostile to the Fathers. This image of Fran-
cisco de Paula Bucareli and his work has been chal-
lenged, however, in a study by the Argentine historian
Julio César González, from which the following text
has been taken.

On September 4, 1767 the Governor of Buenos Aires,
Francisco de Paula Bucareli y Ursúa, wrote to the
Count of Aranda of the difficulties offered by the royal
decree of February 27, relative to the expulsion of the
members of the Society of Jesus and the first measures
adopted in order to effect it. He said it had seemed "least
dangerous to occupy the colleges of Córdoba del Tucumán,
Paraguay, Corrientes, Sante Fe, and Buenos Aires first, and
also to exile from the city those principal citizens who,
united and in league with the Jesuits, formed secret as-
semblies and councils which tended to disturb the peace;
later I will undertake the conquest of the mission towns,
in which I expect to succeed quickly, although they suppose this to be impossible."

The Jesuit historian Father Pablo Hernández has called
"particular attention to the fact that, from the day on
which the Jesuits were expelled from their houses within
the jurisdiction of the three provinces until the day on
which they were notified of the estrangement in the
Guaraní missions, a year or more passed." To be sure, Bucareli left nothing to chance. He availed himself of the
rights of Article VIII of the "Adición a la instrucción
sobre el extrañamiento de los Jesuítas de los dominios de
S. M. por lo tocante a Indias e islas Filipinas," whereby it
was established that "it would be helpful if the Provincial,
or whoever might have his authority, would write precise
orders to the Jesuits, arranging, by the same means, that
those on hand in their colleges may be arrested first; thus
the Provincial may not search for underhanded extensions,
and the missionaries themselves, seeing themselves deprived of their principal help, may be more punctual in the
fulfillment of the order." He did this to facilitate the gathering of the Jesuit missionaries "who are found to be
widely separated by distance." The executor of the ex-

pulsion ought to receive these orders in sealed envelopes "so that they may express nothing more than the recall of the Fathers without mention of the general decree of expulsion."

The methods put in practice in Misiones for the expulsion of the Jesuits, in the judgment of the cited historian, "reveal truly childish fear." We consider that they rather show an understanding of the step which should be taken in the dominions where the activities and ascendancy of the Society were greatest, and where could be feared, more than in any other region, the agitation of the Indians over the retirement of those who had been their guides for one hundred fifty years.

There is nothing more contradictory than the affirmations of Father Hernández concerning the military character of the undertaking of the Governor of Buenos Aires. At one time or another, depending on how it might fit the demands of the moment, he undertook "the conquest of that pretended empire with an armed hand," or "if one must give credit to the lamentations of Bucareli, the forces on which he counted to effect the expulsion were few and in bad condition," when it is not said that "he boasted of great military force with which to expel the Jesuits, who were not going to put up any resistance at all," and then to persist in the same subject in a later work, affirming that Bucareli boasted of "a formidable enterprise." . . .

Bucareli recommended to the Bishop of Buenos Aires, Dr. Manuel Antonio de la Torre, the search for the regular priests who should take upon themselves the instruction of the Indians in the Catholic religion, in accordance to the instructions of Article VI of the "Adición a la Instrucción," which established that "in place of the Jesuits either clerics or monks must be substituted temporarily or permanently."

In the meantime, Father Lorenzo Balda, the Superior of Misiones, had been ordered to send a chief and a mayor from each of the towns at his convenience, "with the idea of examining, by this means, how the Father is thinking, and also, if he obeys and sends them, with that of acquainting them with the benign pity with which the King has

looked on them, taking them out of the slavery and ignorance in which they have been living, and further, so that
they may be used as hostages when it is time to expel
the Fathers and establish the new government. There are
bound to be great difficulties to overcome at that time,
particularly because of not knowing the Indians' language, for the priests, refusing to do as they were told in
repeated orders, decrees, and mandates, never permitted
them to learn Castilian." . . .

By the fourteenth of that same September the thirty
mayors and an equal number of chiefs of the Guaraní villages of Paraná and Uruguay, with their numerous retinue
of Indians, could already be found in the colonial capital,
their presence corresponding to the design we have already
seen. As the first method to gain the trust and sympathy of
the natives, Bucareli resolved to lodge them "with greater
comfort than the Company had previously afforded them;
I shall give them Spanish-style clothes to wear, waiting on
them and treating them in such a way that they might
recognize the improvement in their fortunes, keeping
them here until it is convenient to use them, and I have
prepared the means of removing the priests and putting in
others, thus establishing the new government."

On November 4 he had them hear a solemn Mass sung
by the Bishop in the Cathedral, in the presence of the principal civil and military authorities of the colony, and afterward feted them with a banquet in the fort. In spite of these
attentions and demonstrations, which were made in order
to inspire them with good will, neither that end nor the
friendship of the native delegation was achieved, and it was
recognized that they obeyed "the teaching of those priests
so thoroughly that they did not believe anything I might
say to them."

"The Jesuits acceded quickly to Bucareli's request, sending him the chiefs and mayors, but as they did not trust
his intentions much they had prepared the Guaraní before sending them off, sharpening their natural distrust.
Furthermore, we may recall that the closing of the colleges of the order and the detention of the Jesuits for
their later remission to Buenos Aires were begun on July
third in the capital, the sixth in Montevideo, the twelfth in

Cordoba, the thirteenth in Santa Fe, the twenty-sixth in Corrientes, and the thirtieth in Asunción, by which we must suppose that the order of exile was known in Misiones before the departure of the Guaraní delegation, which would have given the members of the Society more than sufficient reasons to deduce that the motives which impelled Bucareli to enter into direct contact with the principal native elements were to attract their support to himself in order to annul any Jesuit resistance, and to impede any indigenous uprising. . . .

It has been said that Bucareli's delay in carrying out the expulsion in Misiones was due as much to his desire for the cooperation of the Jesuit provincial, since he was described as the "most powerful aid in guaranteeing the peacefulness of the Indians and the obedience of the Fathers," as to the fact that he lacked clerics and regulars with which to replace the Jesuits. This must be the major cause of the delay with which the expulsion was effected in that province; a delay which stands out in comparison with the rapidity and decisiveness with which it was accomplished in Buenos Aires and Tucumán. It is evident that this was not an unrecognized problem for Bucareli. On October 14, 1768, he confessed to the Count of Aranda in an outburst that was undoubtedly sincere that, "amongst the grave difficulties which presented themselves and kept us from putting into effect the removal of the priests and members of the expelled Order . . . which had me in continual agitation and unrest, was that of finding other ecclesiastics who might relieve them, for these are an indispensable requirement, and we could not go ahead with the expulsion without them." . . .

The nature of the work accomplished by Bucareli on the Río de la Plata has allowed the most diverse opinions and the most varied and contradictory comments to descend dizzily about his person. It is unquestionable that his actions as a public servant can be evaluated in very different ways. But with regard to the expulsion of the members of the Society of Jesus, his work was uniform and his proceedings correct for that which he must have understood as right: the faithful fulfillment of the order of expulsion. Bucareli might have belonged to the group in Spain which prepared the blow against the Society. It might even be admitted that his designation to take charge of the government of the Río de la Plata entered into the plan of the anti-Jesuits. But in the area which we are considering he does not show the weaknesses which have always been observed, nor does he deserve the objections which were leveled against his work as governor. At least the most vulnerable points are not those directly related to his commission in Misiones. . . .

It is not a question of revindicating Bucareli, but of revising the concepts and evaluations of the historians who have insisted on the traditional aspects without bothering to ascertain the degree of truth in that which they were affirming. We do not pretend to extol his work as governor, nor to exaggerate his activity in the expulsion. But we realize that, analyzing the process with the unedited documentation which we exhibit, little or nothing of the Bucareli of Father Hernández, for example, remains. . . .

The Jesuit tradition would have required that the Guaraní towns express the pain which the expulsion caused them with great feeling. But as no mark of these manifestations has remained, it is necessary to manufacture for comparison "the cries and sorrows of the departure. As no report of them by an actual witness remains, they can be deduced by what occurred during the year, and by what happened in the Spanish cities. And as on such occasions the simple multitudes are even more prone to sentiment, being usually more attached to those who have been their benefactors, they necessarily experienced such feelings at this time."

On the other hand Elorduy as well as Zavala[1] has made the state of mind of the Indians very clear. "The natives," he says, "give signs which seem to me unmistakable that the expulsion of their old masters is pleasing to them." This sentence is susceptible of interpretation; what Elorduy undoubtedly wanted to point out was that the Indians witnessed the separation of the Jesuits with indiffer-

---

[1] Nicolás de Elorduy and Francisco Bruno de Zavala were two of the Spanish officers and commissioners in charge of the expulsion [ed.].

ence, and assuming that he who is quiet consents, the commissioner wanted to see in that indifferent silence a sign of indigenous support. It would be ingenuous to attempt to interpret Elorduy's reference as an indication of the happiness which the Indians experienced. They felt neither happiness nor pain, but indifference due to incomprehension of the real meaning of the expulsion they were witnessing.

Returning to the commissioner's report, we should agree that the very simplicity with which he notes the native reaction and the lack of any reason to exaggerate the matter give the greatest credibility to his words. Remember that according to the Jesuits the expulsion as practiced by Bucareli has always been an armed penetration, careful in its military aspect, and attentive to the possible subversive machinations of the expelled regulars. Could Elorduy then be considered prudent for telling Bucareli that the towns were tranquil, that their inhabitants pronounced themselves favorable to the expulsion, if in truth the state of the town was unrest and despair over the loss of their old priests, making him fear an uprising?

The problem is more complex than it seems at first impression. It is impossible to pretend that the natives expressed any great pain over the expulsion. They could not have sensed the full extent of the order of Charles III or all its significance. On the other hand, they could not have appreciated that the change of priests was also that of priestly orders. At first all were the same to them, Jesuit and Franciscan, Dominican or Mercedarian. In any case, they must have realized the extent of the change later on when they recognized that the government of the mission was in the hands of a special administrator, and that the priest and his assistant only attended the cultivation of the "spiritual pasture."

We must not discount the intervention of the chiefs and mayors who accompanied Bucareli, and the factor, always impressive, that it was the King who had ordered the replacement of the regulars. . . .

On July 18 Bucareli entered the town of Yapeyú "with all the equipment and ostentation at his command, in order to capture their good will and respect, putting myself at the head of the grenadiers, whose helmets they had never seen, and which aroused great admiration in the Indians," who ran to receive the party at the pass of the river Guay-birabí with music, dancing, and contests.

We understand very well that it is not possible to accept without reservation the anti-Jesuit declarations, inspired by the idea of explaining the dangers of that Society, which Bucareli formulated in his letters to the Count of Aranda. He wanted to impress the Court with the ability which he put into play in order to elude the various inconveniences which the task of the expulsion offered in Misiones. Neither do we believe that his labor was exempt from difficulties, seeing that it is admissible that he could expect the natives to be restless because of the retirement of the priests to whom they were accustomed. If there was actually no incident which might have impeded the task, it was certain, too, that Bucareli had taken action to prevent any outbreak of an opposition movement. Until now we do not possess any other proofs than those provided by Bucareli or the Jesuits, so that we cannot begin to estimate critically the affirmations of one or the other. But we do not believe it an exaggeration to lend an ear to the Governor of Buenos Aires when he tells us that there existed among the natives "that distrust and horror of the Spaniards with which the Jesuits had impressed them, persuading them from the pulpit that we were their vigorous enemies and that the decree was directed at enslaving them and to taking away their possessions, along with their wives and children, reducing them to the greatest misery, so that they would not believe the chiefs and mayors whom I brought with me."

How was Bucareli to dispel this distrust? From the beginning the commissioners in charge of the expulsion were especially urged to use gentle treatment, under the threat of severe punishment for those who disobeyed. The gifts he distributed among the Indians, and the "mayors and chiefs who told them how well they had been treated, showing them their suits and the dresses which they brought for their wives" also exerted their attraction.

It occurs to us that we can note a certain contradiction between the affirmations concerning the Guaraní's tranquility of spirit and carelessness about the retirement of the Jesuits and these declarations by Bucareli about the distrust with which the Indians viewed the actions of the Spaniards. Nevertheless, this seeming discrepancy, which leads one to induce a false interpretation does not exist, for it is indispensable to combine the two, giving the matter its proper explanation.

Concerning the first, we have already said enough so as not to have to insist on the matter. The natives of Misiones neither understood nor were interested in the effects of the expulsion, but it is possible that the teaching of so many years by the Jesuits, warning them of the danger of having anything to do with the Spaniards, kept them alert and distrustful. Then, it should be understood that their points of contact with the Spaniards being few and superficial, both attitudes had their origin in different events. The native suspicion was not the result of the substitution of the Jesuit regime—how was the Indian to comprehend systems of government or the efficiency of one or another religious order?—but was produced by the lack of contact with the Spaniards and the assurances which the regulars had expounded to them time and again, that this relationship was prejudicial to their interests and in the event that it was effected would lead inevitably to the exploitation of the Indian by the white.

This warning, often repeated in their sermons, which would have been intensified by the time of the expulsion, gave place to the state of mind which Bucareli pointed out. It was comprehensible and logical on the part of the Indian, being the product of an action which neither the Governor himself nor his commissioners could attribute to the expulsion *per se*.

Bucareli stayed in Yapeyú for ten days. He demanded rigorous discipline of the troops; he tried to attract the natives, especially the native women . . . ; he advertised the advantages of the new system arising from the expulsion of the Jesuits, made the authority of the King felt and, in order to remind the Indians of their obligation, set up a portrait of Charles III, executing this act with "fit decorum, to the sound of the discharge of guns and artillery," which was repeated in each of the towns as it was occupied. . . .

V

*The Aftermath of
the Expulsion*

17

Constancio Eguía Ruiz

A STAGGERING BLOW
TO EDUCATION

◈◈◈◈◈◈◈◈◈◈◈

*It would probably be very rewarding to study the
consequences of the expulsion of the Jesuits for the
enlightenment in colonial universities. Were the Jesuit
teachers of the last generation mostly diehard defenders of scholasticism or were they, on the contrary, although to a varying degree, the first representatives of
a Catholic enlightenment? Was their removal necessary in order to modernize colonial universities? Or
would the Jesuit "humanists" rather have considera-
bly enriched late-eighteenth-century enlightened academic culture had they not been expelled, instead of
producing only an isolated literature in exile?*

*Such a study still remains to be done, and the task
which the Spanish Jesuit historian Father Constancio
Eguía Ruiz (born 1871) has performed in the text here
reproduced is a less sophisticated one. He simply gives
us some facts illustrating the gap that the expulsion
of the Jesuits left in primary, secondary, and university education and how difficult it was to fill their*

Translated from Constancio Eguía Ruiz, *España y sus misiones
en los países del Plata* (Madrid, 1953); excerpts from pp. 584-
596; reprinted with the permission of Ediciones Cultura His-
pánica.

places. It is a matter of course that the Father is particularly pleased to be able to quote anti-Jesuit witnesses to show the sad state of affairs after 1767.

If the emptiness the Spanish Jesuits left behind them in their missions was characteristic because the missionary inclination of the ancient Paraguayan province was also very marked and characteristic, the deficiency which their enforced absence produced in the territory of their instruction should not be less notable for this reason. Evidently that deficiency must have been felt in America even more than in the motherland. The needs were graver and more insistent, the means of replacement and restoration much less abundant.

How to find personnel and means to supply the sudden lack of so many and such teachers? . . . that was the question which should have been asked before the expulsion of the Fathers. But it was not asked until later, when the problem had no remedy. The question was asked with greater fervor many years later when antijesuitism was already cold and, already tired of so much ignorance and pedagogic idiocy, everyone began to sigh for the return of the old masters, revealing the sad need of them.

Certainly these confessions were not made by Paraguay exclusively. One can hardly take a step through the colonial archives of that period in any of the cities or towns of our continent without tripping over such ingenuous revelations.

Let us turn to Mexico, and we will find that in Durango, capital of New Biscaye, on opening the order for the re-establishment of the Society in the beginning of the nineteenth century the prelate of the diocese began by saying that, in respect to clerical teaching and the sad state it was in, "it has not been possible for their predecessors to remedy it, nor was it possible of old, except for the Society, nor is it for him now, in spite of so many efforts." And the attorney general of the municipal government tells us that "no matter how much effort they expend, they have not been able to put instruction on the same level as the Jesuits did."

In the order concerning the provinces of Yucatán, at the same time, it was made clear that in Campeche, for example, there had not been any grammar schools for more than thirty years after the expulsion of the Jesuits. In Guadalajara, Mexico, although after thirty or more years of lacking the Jesuits they succeeded in establishing a university, the municipality kept calling for the Jesuits, because it was said that "after their expulsion the instruction of the young was never able to return to the flowering state in which they had it, nor could it give the same fruits."

In the capital of Mexico itself, the very rector of the College of San Ildefonso testifies to its decadence in the number and progress of its students, many years after the expulsion of the Jesuits. . . .

In Quito, likewise, the "great, notable loss" which its two colleges suffered with the expulsion of the Jesuits could do no less than damage the instruction of the young. Those colleges, San Gregorio, accredited to give degrees in theology and canonical law, and the seminary of San Luis, were closed for some years even though there were other centers of instruction. In all the rest of the Republic of Ecuador the only schools were those of the Society; schools of Latin grammar and primary learning in Loja, Guayaquil, Ibarra, and Latacunga, and of grammar only in Cuenca and Riobamba. All except the school of grammar in Cuenca disappeared with the expulsion of the Jesuits.

The provincial jurisdiction of these regulars, who spread themselves from Tucumán to the mouth of the Río de la Plata and farther, was abundantly and explicitly acknowledged, even by their own enemies. Soon after the fatuous joy provoked by the expulsion came the laments, necessarily discreet, for that which was irreplaceable.

There are adequate proofs of this in the letters of Manuel Antonio de Latorre, Bishop of Buenos Aires, although at times he seems to pretend the opposite, being a vigorous opponent of the Jesuits. This priest, writing to the King on November 25, 1768, told him the following: "Hitherto, Sire, the Society has run the schools for the instruction of the young." And as a result of their absence the need to replace them became notable, even in the areas which the Jesuits cultivated least exclusively. Furthermore, he says that no one could be found in their halls to modify or contradict properly the Jesuit doctrines, the support of which was deemed a crime against the state, as the Dominicans had no professors, and hardly anyone who could preach a sermon. Thus he begs His Majesty to send teachers from Spain, where so many abounded that in the region of Castile alone there were enough for Buenos Aires, Córdoba, Paraguay, and other points where courses might be established. . . .

Even Abad Illana, Bishop of Córdoba, in spite of having protested in his reports that the Jesuits were not needed and that above all they were pernicious, at last unwillingly discovered the great deficiency their absence made, especially in the schools, for it fell to him to find the means to fulfill a thousand duties which were no longer provided for.

He finally reported about the ministries: "Lacking the Jesuit fathers we lack the workers who brought forth any fruit." And in regard to instruction he expressed himself in this way: "In view of their absence. I do not know what we are to do with the children and youth of these countries. Who is to teach primary school . . . ? The Franciscan fathers do something," he added. But as we can see, the former Salamanca professor could not satisfy himself with this. And he who had uttered so many injustices on other occasions did not lack an argument this time. Even if it were true that the Franciscans had been substituted for the Jesuits in the University of Córdoba, at least for the time being, in many other areas there were no substitutes at all, and in the cities where the Jesuits had had their greatest faculties, as in Buenos Aires and Asunción, twenty years had already passed without the establishment of analogous courses. . . .

It is well known that the Jesuits had hardly arrived at the school of Santiago del Estero at the end of 1586 before they were teaching primary letters there, and that the school was growing, even though the Jesuits had to supply all the children's school needs. At the departure of the old masters, the priest, don Pedro Cortés de Medina, took charge of the school (at least from 1772). But Cortés resigned in a year, and the cleric don Fernando Díaz Ovejero suc-

ceeded him. However, the latter "being very old and un-
qualified by any standards," in 1778, after five years, the
school found itself in "total decadence." It was necessary to
wait until 1793 for that establishment to be resuscitated
under the auspices of the Dominican fathers.

The school of the Society in Córdoba, which subsisted
as an annex to the university until the expulsion of the
Jesuits, was handed over to the Franciscans, and the Bishop
of Córdoba spoke of it as insufficient in the above-
mentioned lamenting letter. In 1786, the Marquis of Sobre-
monte wanted to apply some better remedy, but only in
1807, after the school had been closed for some time, do
we see it arise again as the result of a grant from the
Cabildo. . . .

In Santa Fe, if anywhere, the Jesuits always attended to
the smooth functioning of their schools until the unlucky
year of 1768. Since that date primary instruction (and the
same could be said of Latin) was given truly mortal blows.
It seemed that they confided these courses to the Dominican father, Francisco Jiménez, that same year, in the hopes
of approval from the provincial governor. But seven years
passed and 1774 arrived, and as yet the royal order of 1767
did not rule there, charging school and doctrine for the
youngest, and grammar and Latin for the more advanced.

Note that from 1770 the *Junta de Temporalidades* was
functioning, and its revenues were destined for the schools
as well as for the jails and hospitals. But only in 1774 was
the grave need recognized and was it decreed to endow
various colonial professors. Twenty years later, in 1790,
the principals of the *Temporalidades* were suspended and,
salaries no longer being paid, the youth of Santa Fe was
once more orphaned of instruction. The Mercedarian fathers were temporarily entrusted with the task of teaching,
in 1792, but either because of the apathy of the families or
perhaps economic troubles, this plan did not last long. This
condition, so detrimental to instruction, was prolonged
even beyond the colonial period. For although solutions
were advanced from time to time, they were not helped to
prosper, certainly, by the tumultuous state of the period
around the turn of the century. Thus, from 1813 until 1817
saw no great improvement in the matter of primary in-

struction. As for the chair of Latin, it was not re-established until after the first third of the century.

With respect to Buenos Aires, today an immense city, it is not strange that at the time of the Jesuit expulsion (1767) primary instruction (not to mention secondary education) might feel itself growing notably feeble after the Jesuits were retired. The town had barely 26,000 souls, including Indians, Mestizos, Mulattoes, and Negroes. And it is well known that the Jesuits had been carrying a considerable burden in the area of "schools of reading, writing, and studying" (as they were called then) from 1617, when they agreed with the governors to do so, until 1767. In *La instrucción primaria durante la dominación española* by Juan Probst one can see for oneself the vicissitudes of such public schools before and after the Society.

Bucareli, the fierce executor of the expulsion of the Jesuits, tried falsely and in vain to mitigate the results of that fatal disposition in the educational regime of the future great city in his reports to Court. "According to various testimonies," says Probst, "and above all in the manifestations which were made later in the *Junta Provincial de Temporalidades*, it was evident that no adequate replacement for the Jesuit's teaching could be found." It was just not enough to apply the properties of the old masters more or less faithfully to grants for free classrooms, and to lay premature foundations for royal schools. What was needed was great integrity on the part of the administrators, sufficiency and constancy of instructors, interest in the heads of family and efficient protection of public power. These conditions did not coincide, either in the last years of colonialism or the dawn of national life. The rattle of arms was always a bad counselor to peaceful instruction. . . . Equally bad were the new theories which, as they were abstract and pretentious, were beyond the capabilities of the poor people. Only by dint of peace, experience, and a realistic approach would public education later be able to enter on a somewhat surer course.

18

João Lúcio de Azevedo

THE FATE OF THE INDIANS AFTER THE JESUITS LEFT

◆◇◆◇◆◇◆◇◆◇◆◇◆

*In order to assess the activities of the Jesuits in Ama-
zonas and the importance of their expulsion it is
necessary to know the events that followed 1759. The
Portuguese historian João Lúcio de Azevedo (1855-
1933) was well qualified to write on this topic. He came
to Pará as an immigrant in the early 1870's and lived
there as a book dealer until 1900. Self-taught, he nevertheless acquired a vast and profound knowledge of
Luso-Brazilian history. His books on the Jesuits in Amazonas, originally published in 1901, on Pombal, Father
Vieira, and "Epocas de Portugal económico" belong
to the best products of modern Portuguese historical
writing. Azevedo's view of the controversial Jesuit
subject is a remarkably objective one, although his
literary style is often emotionally loaded.*

Translated from J. Lúcio de Azevedo, *Os jesuítas no Grão-
Pará, suas missões e a colonização* (2nd ed.; Coimbra, 1930),
excerpts from pp. 335-339, 370-381. Printed with the permission
of Universidade de Coimbra.

The law of June 6, 1755, on the liberty of the Indians, although based on principles of sound philosophy and immanent justice, proved once again the futility of the efforts to save the inferior race from total destruction. The new provisions were made in vain as so many others were which had been promulgated before. Not only the ferocity of the invaders but also the communication, through social contact, of their vices and diseases, was a powerful factor of annihilation. As selfish and covetous as the Jesuits' purpose may have been in segregating the Indians from contacts with the outer world, their obstinacy in keeping them ignorant of the white man's language, for the conservation of the race, was a means of defense, perhaps unconscious, but nevertheless the only effective one. Throughout the vastness of the American continent, the only place where the Indian communities prospered, taking from civilization only that which was adequate for their needs, was Paraguay where the Jesuits established their missions. After the indescribable cruelties of the conquerors of Mexico and Peru and at the time when the oppression of the colonists rapidly proceeded in its destructive work in the Portuguese territory, the missionaries of the Society managed to establish, in neutral terrain, a harbor for the remainder of the persecuted race. Forbidden to the covetousness of the foreigners by prohibitive laws and ruled by a benevolent tyranny under which it prospered, the territory of the missions constituted an almost autonomous nation encrusted in the domains of Castile. . . .

According to our concept of human dignity, the humiliating way and the mental tutelage in which the missionaries kept their neophytes is repugnant. The opposite method, however, did not fare better. A comparison of the two systems clearly shows the fatal influence of the European civilization upon the conquered race. The Jesuit system was able to preserve this race from complete annihilation since it was the continuation of the savage's own ways, with their rudimentary communism and a mental state characterized by the combination of the previous pagan beliefs with the new superstitions of Catholicism. Left to themselves, the Indians would little by little return to their forests and to their primitive rudeness, or they would have to succumb by persisting in their relations with the stronger race. From the north to the south of the continent, this was their destiny. In some parts, they were set in a degrading servitude; in others, they were exiled to the outer limits of civilized zones in lands given them only out of mercy. By one way or another, in a short space of time, their total extinction was a fact. . . .

Perhaps the Jesuits had an intuition of this destiny. In all circumstances their main objective was to conceal the converts and to prevent them as much as possible from communicating with the whites. Considering that they were not able to obtain complete segregation in the Grão-Pará, which had been accomplished in Paraguay, they had a powerful assistant in the Regiment of the Missions for this purpose. "No other persons," reads this famous law, "besides the Indians with their families, will be allowed to work or live in the villages." It set the common penalty of whiplashing for the hired hands and exile for the distinguished people as punishment for those who broke it. For a long time this decree had been used for propaganda purposes against the missionaries. It is easy to understand that in the habitual dealings with the free Indians their brutishness would have furnished more than a few occasions for their being taken advantage of by civilized men. Now the saving precept was invalidated by a law, signed on the same date (June 7, 1755) as the declaration of liberties, and with it was promulgated two years later on the twenty-eighth of May, 1757. . . .

Destined for Brazil, the law determined, as had a previous one of 1611, that all gentiles be freed as well as the mestizos of any kind,[1] excepting those born of an African slave mother. It foresaw the need for labor by regulating the hiring of Indians and the rate of their salaries. In order to put a definite end to the old regime and to extinguish the memory of the missions, it ordered that they should take the name of towns or villages, according to the number of people, and should have their mayors, councilors, and offi-

---

[1] The author uses the term *mestiços indios*, which should refer to halfbreeds who grew up in the Indian villages [ed.].

cers of justice chosen, whenever possible, from among the same Indians who resided there. Yet, at the first sound of liberty, it was necessary to see that those who were the object of such solicitude did not abandon their posts, where, by the enforcement of captivity, salary, or the habit of obedience, they still worked. . . .

The transformation was not as the liberal dispositions of the decree of 1755 led one to believe. It may be that Carvalho himself did not believe much in it. His brother, through the knowledge that he had of the Indians, knew well how far they were from being able to comply on their own with all the rights and obligations that follow from complete liberty. The old edifice had been destroyed and all its faults with it, but to substitute it for another which was not equivalent presented much difficulty. The Directory[2] became, in fact, the continuation of the old regime under the administration of a secular officer. Some parts of the old Regiment of the Missions were kept. The Indians were submitted to the same tutelage; and, though there existed in the villages the nominal authority of mayors, of the town council, and of the more distinguished natives, the real power was held by the Portuguese director, who disposed of everything without the least limitation. Due to the lack of trained personnel, this post was held by individuals of the military caste: officers first, going down the scale to corporals. The men who were entrusted to a mission of such great social implication must often have been both ignorant and tyrannical. . . .

Barely had the Jesuits left the missions when the fragile tie that bound the Indians to a simulated civilization was broken. Pombal's reform which declared them to be free and the Directory of Mendonça, which should have been the origin of rapid social and economic progress, did nothing more than to hasten the fall. Upon the departure of the missionaries from the Spanish domains, the same effect was produced, although with different regulations. But this

---

[2] Ordinances issued in 1757 by Governor Francisco Xavier de Mendonça Furtado (Pombal's half-brother), regulating the Indian towns and villages in Pará [ed.].

does not enter our picture: let us look only at what happened in Pará.

A few years after the regime of the missions had been changed, the government of Lisbon sent an officer, with the title of Visitor, to examine the state of the new populations and to verify how the Directory was being executed, as well as to view the results of its application. The experiment was very discouraging indeed. Except in some villages near the capital, desolation was the rule. The Indians fled to their jungles, and the directors, growing rich from the work of the few that stayed, were the main instrument of annihilation of the previously blossoming communities. So stated the Visitor himself, Manuel da Silva Azevedo, later Governor of the Fortress of Sao Julião, to Father Anselmo Eckart. Confiding in the Jesuit, he added that, according to his way of seeing it, only with the readmission of the missionaries would the centers of Indian settlements once more regain the number of people and the obvious prosperity of the old times. Every testimony collected thereafter confirmed that of Da Silva. The facts show that after the departure of the religious their work gradually fell apart. Although imperfect, the work was the result of noble efforts and hard labor, carried on for more than a century. . . .

We owe the most exact picture of the state of the old missions to a magistrate who, having resided a few years in the localities and due to the nature of his work, was in a better position than anyone to furnish us with minute and creditable information: Dr. Antonio José Pestaña da Silva, Justice and General Superintendent of the Indians of the Captaincy of Rio Negro during the years preceding 1772. The regime was still relatively new; yet already the general failure of the Indian settlements, to which so much progress had been prophesied, was manifest, and the promised liberty was no different from the old slavery, save in showing itself to be perhaps still harder.

Instead of applying themselves to the farming of the lands that belonged to them in the settlements, the Indians wandered from one place to another. At the Director's bidding they performed various tasks which he arbitrarily gave them. This was the background of the desolation and progressive decadence of the areas. . . .

In spite of all the measures of theoretical protection contained in the laws, the relations between whites and Indians continued to be as oppressive for the latter as they had been before, perhaps even more so. The so-called towns or villages were ruled without any limitation by the will of the Director, as a rule a brutal and violent man, almost always a soldier and frequently of the lowest rank. "These officers," informed the quoted justice, "have assumed all coercive jurisdiction and make their houses the jails and scaffolds of the Indians." In cases where the Governor had been persuaded to allow some of them to be sent to serve in private farms, they were made to work more than human strength can endure. If they fell asleep from excess fatigue, pepper was dropped in their eyes to awaken them. If they fled the hardship of labor and bad treatment, they were condemned to do labor with foot-shackles in the public works. They were not allowed to choose their masters or to discuss their payment. They went to the house to which they were assigned for their miserable salary which, according to the table at the time of Mendonça, was two sticks of cloth per month, then worth 300 *réis*. Many times they were made to leave the benevolent master whom they served with pleasure only to be delivered to another whom, by his inhumanity, they hated beforehand. This led the same justice to say, "If this form or procedure is not captivity, there can be nothing that destroys liberty more at its root."

All this generated the depopulation. The existing centers did not increase; on the contrary, they decreased ostensibly. From outside, no new elements came in, and the deserters grew in number, frightening off with the stories they told the wandering tribes to regions always more remote. Some of the Indians that remained nearby were ferocious and irreducible, such as the Muras, who did not spare even their fellow Indians, killing them during their trips and in the villages. During these assaults, either as aggressors or victims, they contributed to the annihilation of the race.

In this case the need for the missionaries cannot be denied. By themselves, through kindness and persuasion, the missionaries domesticated even the most savage Indians; or working through those they had already attracted, they convinced the others to come and participate in the comforts of civilization.

What a difference from the times when La Condamine, coming down from Quito, admired the comfort and state of relative progress of the Indians in the Portuguese missions! "We began to see," says the French scholar, "in place of houses and churches made only of straw, chapels and presbyteries of stone and clay, of adobe and brick, and the walls very well whitewashed. We also saw, with pleasant surprise, in the middle of these deserts the Indian women all with their Breton shirts, and in the houses, chests with iron locks, needles, mirrors, knives, scissors, combs, and various other objects from Europe. . . . The commerce which they maintain with Pará gives these Indians and their missionaries an air of plenty, which at first sight immediately distinguishes the Portuguese missions from the Spanish." In those far-off places priests of Carmel and of the Society of Jesus, vying with each other, promoted along with religious education the material well-being of their converts. The missionaries, we well know, enriched with the work of their pupils the communities to which they belonged. At the same time they increased, with new elements, the benefits of their action. . . .

As it was impossible to recall the Jesuits, the only ones capable or renewing the work of catechesis with the previous success, the Queen accepted the proposal of the Governor of Pará, Francisco de Sousa Coutinho, for the reorganization of the civilizing task. With this objective, the Directory was abolished. The Indians were put on equal footing with others under the law. Thus the oppressive tutelage to which they had been subjected was extinguished. It was determined that the contracts for the hiring of service should be made by mutual agreement of the parties involved. Once more the raids and offensive wars against the Indians were prohibited. To attract the savage population, the law determined that guides and people who crossed the jungles should carry along gifts to distribute among the Indians. With this lure, the Indians should be invited to enjoy the advantages of a comfortable life near the whites. But the characteristic aspect of the new structure consisted of grouping the Indians into a militia corps whose officers would be, without distinction, the principal Indians and the whites who were residents of the villages. Under such an order, the change of the primitive system could not have been more radical: via the Directory, the savage groups passed from the theocratic regime to the military—the captain replaced the religious, the soldier substituted the catechist.

It does not require deep insight to realize that such an organization could not favor liberty. The Queen's decree changed the legal statutes, but did not alter the situation of the Indians. The military regime, by its very nature tyrannical, facilitated oppression against which the rudeness, timidity, and the habit of humble obedience of the natives made it impossible for them to react. . . .

Therefore, the causes that had given rise to the desertion and which had destroyed the race continued to exist. Of the many measures that had been ordered into effect to protect the Indians since the time of the kings of Castile,[3] not one was effective in practice. Only the system of the Jesuits had been successful, now destroyed. In addition to opposition by the colonists, the system suffered from the same faults that had overthrown the Society of Jesus. It established a state within a state; it provoked covetousness in the missionaries themselves which in turn increased the hostility between them and the civil power.

Even if we discount some of the writings in the chronicles due to exaggeration, it is irrefutable that in the beginning the Indian population was numerous, at least along the coastline and along the margins of the rivers. When the first explorers ran over the coasts everywhere they landed savages came to meet them, sometimes in admiration and other times in hostility. The wonder of Tomé de Sousa, manifest in the characteristic words we have already quoted: "They

[3] A reference to the period of Spanish-Portuguese Union, 1580-1640 [ed.].

are so many that were they to be cut in a butcher shop there would never be a shortage," and the reports of the raids of the invaders, counting by the thousands the dead and the prisoners, are valuable as detailed statistics. In the immense basin of the Amazon, along the beaches or in the highlands, the human clusters were spread like anthills, and the space that separated them along the main arteries was relatively short, especially if we compare them to the deserts that we find today. . . .

Of all the villages that the margins of the Amazon offered to the sight of its first discoverer, perhaps not one modern settlement marks their place. The hundred fifty tribes which then existed in this area have all disappeared. Not only that, the centers of population have grown little in number. Further, if we exclude the main cities, the number of inhabitants of all races does not exceed by much the population of the Indian villages at the time of the missionaries. . . .

In the central part of the continent, in the wide zone that stretches out between the most densely populated strip along the coast and the foot of the Andes, and in places which civilized men do not walk on, the numerous tribes still wander. Closer to the reach of the invader, and decimated by contact with them, are stationed the rest of the Jurunas, Mundurucús, Maúes, Parintintins, Catauixis, and other members of the Tupi family, constituting small groups of refugees, instead of the bellicose nations which they formed before. These relics of the ancient masters of the continent still exist for the sole reason that the explorations into the interior of the territory remained practically at a standstill. . . .

Once the missionary had been expelled and the attempts of the slave hunters had been restrained out of respect for the laws which the harsh regime of Pombal had been able to inculcate, there was a lack of incentive for discovery. Little by little the vacuum around civilization became wider and all contact ceased between it and the primitive Indians. Still the tradition was renewed in this century, and some occasional attempts are now made to civilize the Indians by means of missions. But many of the missionaries lack the enthusiasm and authority of their Jesuit predecessors. The result of the experiment has been nil until now, and the savages continue to live relatively in peace in their faraway places. . . .

APPENDIX

The Curriculum Vitae
of a Jesuit Missionary

Many, if not most, of the Jesuit missionaries in Latin America whose names have become famous were foreigners such as Eusebio Kino, Samuel Fritz, Anton Sepp, Florian Paucke, and Martin Dobritzhoffer. Their writings in some cases constituted unique sources of knowledge about America all over Europe. Nevertheless, the great majority of the missionaries were Spaniards, Portuguese, or native Americans—and in many cases very remarkable men, too. For an example we choose Father José Cardiel, an indefatigable missionary who personifies the Jesuit efforts in their most famous field of action, the region of the River Plate.[1]

One of three brothers, all of whom joined the Society of Jesus, José Cardiel was born in the Spanish province of Rioja in 1704. Having entered the order in 1720, he came to the River Plate nine years later. Soon we find him in the Guaraní missions, where he was to stay for about ten years. When the Guaraní troops were ordered by Governor Bruno Zavala to subdue the Paraguayan rebellion in 1734, Cardiel accompanied them as a chaplain. During most of the 1740's this Jesuit, who was obviously bursting with a tremendous energy that did not get an outlet in the stabilized and calm Guaraní community, was employed in various ambitious missionary and exploration enterprises. He was engaged in the first efforts to pacify and christen the warlike Abipones and Charrúas, and he dreamed of exploring the whole of Patagonia down to the Straits of Magellan, winning the roaming hordes of natives for Christ. His expeditions in the unknown South with fellow missionaries

[1] The account is based on G. Furlong, *José Cardiel, S.J. y su Carta-Relación (1747)* (Buenos Aires, 1953) and on Cardiel's own writings.

José Quiroga and the English convert Thomas Falkner were remarkable feats even if Cardiel's ambitions were far from being realized.

He also found time to write down detailed and valuable accounts of his experiences, both in Patagonia and in the Guaraní missions. In the beginning of the 1750's he was again assigned a post in these missions, the time when the Border Treaty of 1750 caused a profound shock in Jesuit quarters. Father Cardiel certainly belonged to the leaders of the Jesuit opposition against the treaty. Even when the General of the order sent a personal representative to "Paraguay" to help the Spanish-Portuguese boundary commission overcome the resistance of the missionaries, José Cardiel insisted in the iniquity of ceding the seven southern missions to the Portuguese, which rendered him disciplinary punishment from his superiors. He now had to change his behavior and soon he was active in assisting the Spaniards in evacuating the recalcitrant Indians from the seven missions. But in the literary field he continued his fight. Cardiel's excellent refutation of Pombal's *Relação Abbreviada* was published in 1901 under the title *Declaración de la verdad* (Statement of the Truth). He was perhaps the Jesuit chiefly responsible for having made the new Spanish Governor, Pedro Ceballos, a loyal friend of the missionaries and a foe of the Portuguese. After the Border Treaty was annulled in 1761, war broke out between the two countries and Ceballos made a victorious expedition into Portuguese territory with his troops. He was accompanied by Father Cardiel.

At the moment of the expulsion, the old Jesuit was once again among his Guaraní. As distinguished from many fellow missionaries, he survived the long journey from Buenos Aires to Spain and, finally, Italy, where like most "Paraguayans" he took up his residence in the little town of Faenza. All the Jesuits received a pension from the Spanish state, obviously a very meager one. Cardiel, whose health was now broken, suffered a great deal in his new surroundings. Probably in 1771 he composed his best-known opus, a *Breve relación* (short account) of the Guaraní missions, published by Father Pablo Hernández in his *Organización social . . .* in 1913. It shows the mission community at its height, in full detail. It is interesting to compare this with another account on the same topic, a *Carta Relación* written by Cardiel in 1747 and published by Father Guillermo Furlong in Buenos Aires in 1953. When Cardiel wrote the earlier account, the future of the missions still seemed a bright and promising one. Besides writing (not very extensively in comparison with many of his brethren), Father Cardiel was also a diligent map-maker. His last years in Italy were mainly devoted to this occupation, perhaps as important from a historical point of view as his writings. He died in 1782.

The obituary testimony of a missionary usually runs that he was humble, zealous, and devout; Cardiel, too, has been thus described. But other traits in his character can be discerned as well: a fiery, restless spirit, a courage which was moral as well as physical, a frankness which must often have been on the harsh side. "Both his words and letters breathe fire," a contemporary said.

A Short Chronology

1756   The Guaraní rebellion subdued by Spanish and Portu-
          guese troops
1757   Pombal deprives Jesuits of their influence at the Portu-
          guese Court; first Jesuit missionaries expelled from
          Amazonas
1759   Attempt on the life of the Portuguese king; all Jesuits in
          the Portuguese dominions expelled or imprisoned
1761   Missionary Malagrida burned at stake in Lisbon; Border
          Treaty annulled
1764   Jesuit Order suppressed in France
1765   A papal bull eulogizes the Jesuits for the last time
1766   "Hat and Cloak Riots" in Spain provide the pretext for
          the expulsion of the Jesuits
1767   Jesuits expelled from all the dominions of Spain
1768   Jesuits leave the missions of Paraguay
1773   Society of Jesus dissolved by the papal bull *Dominus ac
          Redemptor*
1814   Society of Jesus reestablished by the Pope

A Bibliographical Note

The literature on the Jesuit order in extensive. There is an abundance of collections of documents, of polemical publications for and against the Jesuits, of chronicles and of modern interpretations. So far as bibliographical tools are concerned A. & A. Backer & C. Sommervogel, *Bibliothèque de la Compagnie de Jésus,* 10 vols. (Paris, 1890-1909) and Robert Streit, *Bibliotheca missionum,* 21 vols. (Munster, Aachen, 1916-1955) deserve to be especially mentioned. Since 1932 there have been excellent annual bibliographical surveys in the review *Archivum Historicum Societatis Iesu* (Rome). A classic work on Jesuit history is J. Crétineau-Joly, *Histoire religieuse, politique et littéraire de la Compagnie de Jésus,* 6 vols. (Paris, 1844-1846). The best Protestant account is Heinrich Boehmer, *Die Jesuiten,* 3rd ed. (Leipzig, Berlin, 1913); among Catholic ones may be mentioned: T. J. Campbell, *The Jesuits, 1534-1921* (New York, 1921) and R. García Villoslada, *Manual de historia de la Compañía de Jesús,* 2nd ed. (Madrid, 1954). A more popular account stressing intellectual activities is René Fülöp-Miller, *The Power and Secret of the Jesuits,* transl. (Garden City, N.Y., 1930 and in a new paperback ed.). Finally, L. von Pastor's monumental work *The History of the Popes from the Close of the Middle Ages,* transl., 38 vols. (St. Louis, Mo., 1950), contains abundant material on Jesuit history.

Modern Jesuit scholars have been very busy publishing the basic documentary material that is kept mainly in the central archives of the Order in Rome. The series *Monumenta Historica Societatis Iesu* (Madrid, 1894-1919; Rome, 1932-   ) now comprises 90 thick volumes. Of special interest to the Latin-Americanist are the chronologically arranged subsections *Monumenta Mexicana,* ed. by Félix Zubillaga; *Monumenta Peruana,* ed. by Antonio de Egaña;

and *Monumenta Brasiliæ*, ed. by Serafim Leite. None has yet reached the seventeenth century. During the present century "official" Jesuit histories on most major regions have been published. Although unavoidably somewhat biased, they represent good scholarship. Of interest are Francisco Rodrigues, *História da Companhia de Jesus na Assistencia de Portugal*, 4 vols. (Porto, 1931-1950) and Antonio Astrain, *Historia de la Compañía de Jesús en la Asistencia de España*, 7 vols. (Madrid, 1912-1925).

In the case of Brazil a monumental work by a modern Jesuit scholar, Serafim Leite, *História da Companhia de Jesus no Brasil*, 10 vols. (Lisbon, Rio de Janeiro, 1938-1950), covers the whole subject. Jesuit history in Brazil centers around three great figures: Nóbrega, Anchieta, and Vieira. Nóbrega's missionary methods have been criticized recently by the sociologist Gilberto Freyre (see page 23) and by Mecenas Dourado, *A conversão do gentio* (Rio de Janeiro, 1958). On his principal fellow missionary see Helen G. Dominian, *Apostle of Brazil: the Biography of Padre José de Anchieta, S.J., 1534-1597* (New York, 1958). The principal work on Vieira is João Lúcio de Azevedo, *História de António Vieira*, 2 vols., 2nd ed. (Lisbon, 1918-1920). Other more recent studies are Maxime Haubert, *L'église et la défense des sauvages: le Père Antoine Vieira au Brésil* (Brussels, 1964) and Charles R. Boxer, *A Great Luso-Brazilian Figure, Padre António Vieira, 1608-1697* (London, 1957). His *Cartas* have been edited by De Azevedo in 3 vols. (Coimbra, 1925-1928). The fight between colonists and Jesuits in Amazonas is recorded in a contemporary Jesuit chronicle by J. F. Bettendorf, *Chronica da missão dos padres da Companhia de Jesus no estado de Maranhão* (Rio de Janeiro, 1910), by De Azevedo, *Os jesuítas no Grão-Pará, suas missões e a colonização*, 2nd ed. (Coimbra, 1930); and by M. C. Kiemen, *The Indian Policy of Portugal in the Amazon Region, 1614-1693* (Washington, D.C., 1954).

Pombal's bitter pamphlet *Relação abbreviada da Republica que os religiosos jesuítas das províncias de Portugal e Hespanha estabeleceram nos dominios ultramarinos . . .* (Lisbon, 1757) has been published in several languages. Besides Gonzaga Jaeger's account and Visconde de Carnaxide's book, both quoted in this volume, there are two other works of interest in this connection: António P. C. Fernandes, *Missionários jesuítas no Brasil no tempo de Pombal*, 2nd ed. (Porto Alegre, 1941) and Marcos Carneiro Mendonça, *O Marques de Pombal e o Brasil* (São Paulo, 1960). The latter is a collection of documents.

The Jesuits' first contacts with Spanish America are dealt with by Francisco Mateos, "Antecedentes de la entrada de los jesuítas españoles en las misiones de América (1538-1565), *Missionalia Hispanica*, I, no. 1/2 (Madrid, 1944), and F. Zubillaga, *La Florida. La misión jesuítica (1566-1572) y la colonización española* (Rome, 1941). The classic work on Mexican Jesuit history is Francisco Xavier Alegre, *Historia de la Compañía de Jesús en la Nueva España*, 3 vols. (Mexico, 1841-1842 and later ed. by E. Burrus). An even more famous historian among the ex-Jesuits of New Spain was Francisco Xavier Clavijero, whose *Storia antica del Messico* has also been published in other languages. Modern histories by Jesuit scholars include Mariano Cuevas, *Historia de la Iglesia en México*, 5 vols. (Mexico, 1946-1947) and Gerard Decorme, *La obra de los jesuítas mexicanos durante la época colonial, 1572-1767*, 2 vols. (Mexico, 1941). On teaching activities see J. V. Jacobsen, *Educational Foundations of the Jesuits in Sixteenth Century New Spain* (Berkeley, Calif., 1938) and D. E. López Sarrelangue, *Los colegios jesuítas de la Nueva España* (Mexico, 1941). With regard to a famous feud, see Genaro García, *Don Juan de Palafox y Mendoza, obispo de Puebla* . . . (Mexico, 1918). A rich literature exists on the Jesuit missionary enterprise in northwestern New Spain. Several monographs by the Jesuit Peter Masten Dunne should be kept in mind. Another contribution is J. F. Bannon, *The Mission Frontier in Sonora, 1620-1687* (New York, 1955). Herbert Bolton, author of an article quoted in the present volume, also wrote the important work, *The Rim of Christendom: a Biography of Eusebio Francisco Kino, Pacific Coast Pioneer* (New York, 1936). Bolton also edited *Kino's Historical Memoir of Pimería Alta*, 2 vols. (Cleveland, 1919), while *Kino Reports to Headquarters: Correspondence from New Spain with Rome* was published by the Institute of Jesuit History in Rome in 1954.

In Central America the Jesuits were mainly active as educators. John Tate Lanning, *The University in the Kingdom of Guatemala* (Ithaca, N.Y., 1955), highlights some of their activities.

The classic Jesuit work on Venezuela is missionary Joseph Gumilla's *El Orinoco ilustrado*, ed. by C. Bayle (Madrid, 1945). See also M. Aguirre Elorriaga, *La Compañía de Jesús en Venezuela* (Caracas, 1941). Among the Jesuits of New Granada, Alonso de Sandoval, who was a less-known colleague of Pedro Claver as an apostle of the Negro slaves, wrote a work called *De instauranda aethiopum salute*, reissued in Bogotá in 1956. On the Indian missions the classic work is Juan Rivero, *Historia de las misiones de los llanos de Casanare y los ríos Orinoco y Meta* (Bogotá, 1956).

Famous Jesuit chronicles on regions farther south include José Chantre y Herrera, *Historia de las misiones de la Compañía de Jesús en el Marañón español* (Madrid, 1901) and José Velasco, *Historia moderna del Reino de Quito y crónica de la Provincia de la Compañía de Jesús* (Quito, 1941). A modern Jesuit history on the province of Quito was published by J. Jouanen (Quito, 1941-1943). How a German Jesuit defended Spanish interests is told in G. Edmundson (ed.), *Journal of the Travels and Labours of Father Samuel Fritz, S.J., in the River of the Amazonas between 1686 and 1723* (London, 1922). The most famous Jesuit in Peru was probably the missionary José de Acosta (died 1600). His *Obras*, ed. by F. Mateos, appeared in Madrid in 1954. The works of another Jesuit chronicler of Peru, Bernabé Cobo, also appeared there in 1956. A modern survey is Rubén Vargas Ugarte, *Los jesuítas del Perú, 1568-1767* (Lima, 1943). Alonso de Ovalle's *Histórica relación del Reyno de Chile, y de las misiones y ministerios que ejercita en él la Compañía . . .* , originally published in 1646 with an English edition in 1649, was reprinted in Santiago in 1888.

On the Paraguayan province of the Order, comprising the whole of the River Plate region and part of present Bolivia, and particularly on the Guaraní missions, the literature is abundant indeed. Excerpts from the documentation in the Archivo de Indias in Seville have been published by

P. Pastells (and F. Mateos) as *Historia de la Compañía de Jesús en la Provincia del Paraguay* . . . , 8 vols. [the last one in two parts] (Madrid, 1912-1959). See also F. Mateos, "La Colección Pastells de documentos sobre América y Filipinas," *Revista de Indias*, VIII, no. 27 (Madrid, 1947). The *Cartas Anuas* of the province for the period 1609-1637, ed. by C. Leonhardt, appeared in two volumes (Buenos Aires, 1927-1929). Among several contemporary chroniclers the most famous were Pedro Lozano, author of *Historia de la Conquista del Paraguay, Río de la Plata y Tucumán*, 5 vols. (Buenos Aires, 1873-1875) and other works, and P. F. J. de Charlevoix, *Histoire du Paraguay*, 3 vols. (Paris, 1756, with an English ed. in 1769). The ex-Jesuit Bernardo Ibáñez de Echávarri in his *Reino Jesuítico* (Madrid, 1770) gave the classic blackening of the missions: see Furlong's study in *Archivum Historicum S.I.*, II (1933). Other famous eyewitness accounts of mission life include those of A. Ruiz de Montoya, José Cardiel, and the Germans Anton Sepp, Martin Dobritzhoffer, and Florian Paucke. On the part of Jesuit scholars the basic works are Pablo Hernández, *Organización social de las doctrinas guaraníes de la Compañía de Jesús*, 2 vols. (Barcelona, 1913) and Guillermo Furlong, *Misiones y sus pueblos de guaraníes* (Buenos Aires, 1962).

Of the many books in German on the missions, the best one is Maria Fassbinder, *Der "Jesuitenstaat" in Paraguay* (Halle, 1926); among the French ones may be mentioned C. Lugon, *La république communiste chretienne des guaranis, 1610-1768* (Paris, 1949); in English, besides R. B. Cunninghame Graham's book quoted in this volume, Magnus Mörner, *The Political and Economic Activities of the Jesuits in the La Plata Region. The Hapsburg Era* (Stockholm, 1953); and, finally, in Portuguese, Aurelio Porto, *História das missões orientais do Uruguai*, 2nd ed., 2 vols. (Porto Alegre, 1954). Special aspects are dealt with by O. Quelle, "Das Problem des Jesuitenstaates Paraguay," *Ibero-Amerikanisches Archiv*, VIII (Berlin, 1934) and M. Mörner, "The Guaraní Missions and the Segregation Policy of the Spanish Crown," *Archivum Historicum S.I.*, XXX (Rome, 1961).

The relations between the Spanish Jesuit missions of

the Paraguayan province of the Order and their Brazilian neighbors have been of great historical importance. Documents on this subject from the Angelis collection of the Biblioteca Nacional, Rio de Janeiro, have been published under titles of *Jesuítas e bandeirantes no Guairá, . . . no Itatim, . . . no Paraguai* (Rio, 1951-1955). See also M. Mörner, "Os Jesuítas espanhois, as suas Missões Guarani e a rivalidade luso-espanhola pela Banda Oriental, 1715-1737," *Revista Portuguesa de História,* IX (Coimbra, 1960). Documents on the fateful Border Treaty of 1750 have been published by the Archivo General of Argentina (1931) and by the Biblioteca Nacional of Brazil (1938). Further documentation can be found in Jaime Cortesão (ed.), *Alexandre de Gusmão e o tratado de Madri,* 5 parts (Rio, 1950). Besides a series of articles on the treaty and the Guaraní war by F. Mateos in *Missionalia Hispanica,* V (1948)-XI (1954) and *Miscelánea Americanista,* III (Madrid, 1952), the principal work is Guillermo Kratz, *El tratado hispano-portugués de límites de 1750 y sus consecuencias* (Rome, 1954). Both these authors are Jesuits. See also D. Ramos Pérez, *El tratado de límites de 1750 y la expedición de Iturriaga al Orinoco* (Madrid, 1946).

It is always interesting to compare developments in Spanish America during the colonial period with those in the Philippines. H. de la Costa, *The Jesuits in the Philippines, 1581-1768* (Cambridge, Mass., 1961) is a detailed account by a Jesuit scholar.

The important role played by non-Spanish Jesuits has been dealt with by Lázaro Aspurz, *La aportación extranjera a las misiones españolas del Patronato Regio* (Madrid, 1946); V. Sierra, *Los jesuítas germanos en la conquista espiritual de Hispano América* (Buenos Aires, 1944) and by M. Batllori in an essay in *The Americas,* XIV, No. 4 (Washington, 1958). The view of an anthropologist on the Jesuit missions is expressed by A. Métraux in a chapter in the *Handbook of South American Indians,* V (Washington, 1949), in "Le caractère de la conquête jésuitique," *Acta Americana,* I (Austin, Tex., 1943), and in his article "The contribution of the Jesuits to the exploration and anthropology of South America," *Mid-América* (a Jesuit historical journal), XXVI (Chicago, Ill., 1944). On economic administration see F. Chevalier (ed.), *Instrucciones a los hermanos jesuítas administradores de haciendas* (Mexico, 1950).

The expulsion of the Jesuits from Spain has been described by William Coxe, *Memoirs of the Kings of Spain of the House of Bourbon* . . . , 2nd ed., Vol. IV (London, 1815) and in the histories of Charles III by A. Ferrer del Río, M. Danvila y Collado, and François Rousseau, as well as by R. Altamira y Crevea in his history of Spain. Important antecedents are highlighted in *Correspondencia reservada e inédita del P. F. de Rávago, confesor de Fernando VI*, ed. by C. Pérez Bustamante (Madrid, 1936). See also C. Eguía Ruiz, *Los jesuitas y el motín de Esquilache* (Madrid, 1947).

A *Colección general de las providencias hasta aquí tomadas por el gobierno sobre el estrañamiento y ocupación de temporalidades de los regulares de la Compañía* . . . was published in 5 vols. in Madrid (1767-1784). A similar collection regarding the River Plate was published by F. J. Bravo (Madrid, 1872), who also edited *Inventarios de los bienes hallados, a la expulsión de los Jesuítas* . . . *en los pueblos de Misiones fundados en las márgenes del Uruguay y Paraná* . . . (Madrid, 1872). Other similar collections include V. Rico González, *Documentos sobre la expulsión de los jesuítas y ocupación de sus temporalidades en Nueva España, 1772-1783* (Mexico, 1949) and A. F. Pradeau, *La expulsión de los jesuítas de las provincias de Sonora, Ostimuri y Sinaloa en 1767* (Mexico, 1959). In A. Carayon, *Charles III et les jésuites de ses états d'Europe et d'Amérique en 1767. Documents inédits* (Paris, 1868) three Jesuit relations on the expulsion from Spanish America have been published. A well-known monograph is Pablo Hernández, *El extrañamiento de los jesuítas del Río de la Plata* . . . (Madrid, 1908; Col. de libros y documentos ref. a la historia de América, VII). His pro-Jesuit interpretation has been challenged by Julio C. González in "Notas para una historia de los treinta pueblos de Misiones, I-II," *Anuario de Historia Argentina*, 1942-1943/1945 (Buenos Aires, 1943-1947). See also J. M. Mariluz Urquijo, "Los guaraníes después de la expulsión de los jesuítas," *Estudios Americanos*, VI, No. 25 (Sevilla, 1953). For the economic aspect see L. M. Torres, "La administración de temporalidades en el Río de la Plata," *Revista de la Universidad de Buenos Aires*, XXXV (1917) and E. Fontana, "La expulsión de los jesuítas de Mendoza y sus repercusiones económicas," *Revista Chilena de Historia y Geografía*, CXXX (1962).

On the cultural activities of the exiled Jesuits see José Toribio Medina, *Noticias bio-bibliográficas de los jesuítas expulsos de América en 1767* (Santiago, 1914); a chapter on "Eighteenth Century Jesuitic Humanism" in M. Picón Salas, *A Cultural History of Spanish America*, transl. (Berkeley, Los Angeles, 1963); A. Gerbi, *Viejas polémicas sobre el Nuevo Mundo* (Lima, 1944) and Bernabé Navarro's essay, "Los jesuítas y la Independencia," *Abside: Revista de Cultura Mexicana*, XV (Mexico, 1952). While the relation between Suárez' thinking and Expulsion and Independence has been studied by M. Giménez Fernández, *Las doctrinas populistas en la Independencia de Hispano-América* (Seville, 1947) and in several works by G. Furlong (one of them quoted in this volume) the rumors of Jesuit conspiracies were scrutinized by Boleslao Lewin, *La supuesta participación jesuítica en la rebelión de Túpac Amaru* (Cochabamba, 1948) and Miguel Batllori, *El Abate Viscardo: historia y mito de la intervención de los jesuítas en la Independencia de Hispanoamérica* (Caracas, 1953). The interesting story of an Argentine Jesuit who returned from exile in 1799 and was a witness to the emancipation is told by Guillermo Furlong in his *Diego León Villafañe y su "Batalla de Tucumán" (1812)* (Buenos Aires, 1962).

In spite of the enormous amount of literature existing on Jesuit history, it may be added that a great deal of unpublished sources of Jesuit origin, many of them scarcely touched by research still are to be found in the archives of Europe and Latin America. It used to be very difficult for non-Jesuits to gain admission to the Central Archives of the Order in Rome, but it is now much easier. Although a great part of the Jesuit archives, confiscated in 1759 and 1767, has unfortunately perished, other parts can be consulted in different archives of Latin America and of the Iberian peninsula. See F. Mateos, "La Colección Bravo de documentos jesuíticos sobre América," *Missionalia Hispanica*, XX, No. 59 (Madrid, 1963), pp. 129-175, and

C. Eguía Ruiz, "Dispersión total de papeles jesuíticos en España," *Hispania*, XI (Madrid, 1951), pp. 679-702. A great part of the unprinted Jesuitica is available on microfilm. See J. F. Bannon, "The Saint Louis University Collection of Jesuitica Americana," *Hispanic American Historical Review*, XXXVII (1957), pp. 82-88.

A NOTE ON THE TYPE

The text of this book was set on the Linotype in Janson, a recutting made direct from type cast from matrices long thought to have been made by the Dutchman Anton Janson, who was a practicing type founder in Leipzig during the years 1668–87. However, it has been conclusively demonstrated that these types are actually the work of Nicholas Kis (1650–1702), a Hungarian, who most probably learned his trade from the master Dutch type founder Dirk Voskens. The type is an excellent example of the influential and sturdy Dutch types that prevailed in England up to the time William Caslon developed his own incomparable designs from these Dutch faces.